Turning Points

Unlocking the Treasures of the Church

JAMES PHILIPPS

TWENTY THIRD 23rd PUBLICATIONS

Dedication

To all of the young people I have had the privilege of knowing.
You are the Church of the third millennium.

To those who have caught a glimpse of that future, especially:
Sr. Lauren Hanley, Ms. Gwen Costello, Fr. Thomas Bonacci,
and Mr. James Boglioli.

Twenty-Third Publications
A Division of Bayard
One Montauk Avenue, Suite 200
PO Box 6015
New London, CT 06320
(860) 437-3012
(800) 321-0411
www.23rdpublications.com

The Scripture passages contained herein are from the *New Revised Standard Version of the Bible,* copyright ©1989, by the Division of Christian Education of the National Council of Churches of Christ in the U.S.A. All rights reserved.

ISBN-10: 1-58595-577-9
ISBN 978-1-58595-577-0
Library of Congress Catalog Card Number: 2005936958
Printed in the U.S.A.

Acknowledgments

I would like to thank many at Twenty-Third Publications for their continued support and encouragement of my work. In particular, I am grateful to Gwen Costello for giving me the preliminary OK for this book during her tenure as publisher and for her hands-on editing of the manuscript. Thanks to Bill Huebsch for his enthusiastic support of this project in its later phases and to Mary Carol Kendzia for her help in shepherding this manuscript (and me!) through the editing process and answering any questions I may have had. Thanks to Michelle Gerstel for her copyediting skills.

I am grateful to my good friend Tony Ercolano for time and time again lending a compassionate ear and insightful observation as we worked together in ministry. Tony and Margaret, *ad multos annos.* Thanks to the members of the Religious Education Department at Holy Trinity High School—in particular my chairperson, Tony Marinelli—for their continued willingness to share their thoughts, opinions, and knowledge with me.

I thank my wife, Rosalie, and my children for their honest appraisals of my work and for putting up with those times when my pontificating at the dinner table about, say, the effects of the Council of Trent, probably exceeded the realms of polite conversation!

Lastly, I am indebted to my students—teenage and adult—for sharing their thoughts on what an authentic experience of Church feels like and for their faith-filled reflections on the tumultuous times since the Vatican Council II. You are often my touchstones to a saner, more authentic encounter with Christ when my own frustrations get the best of me.

Contents

Introduction

> Jesus left that place and went away to the district of Tyre and Sidon. Just then a Canaanite woman from that region came out and started shouting, "Have mercy on me, Lord, Son of David; my daughter is tormented by a demon." But he did not answer her at all. And his disciples came and urged him, saying, "Send her away, for she keeps shouting after us." He answered, "I was sent only to the lost sheep of the house of Israel." But she came and knelt before him, saying, "Lord, help me." He answered, "It is not fair to take the children's food and throw it to the dogs." She said, "Yes, Lord, yet even the dogs eat the crumbs that fall from their masters' table." Then Jesus answered her, "Woman, great is your faith! Let it be done for you as you wish." And her daughter was healed instantly. (Matthew 15:21–28)

It's an amazing story. Here is Jesus, the good shepherd, wonder-worker extraordinaire, refusing to heal. His mission as he understands it is clear: go to the lost sheep of the house of Israel—that is, to other Jews who are in need of physical and spiritual healing. Given the enormity of this task, Jesus doesn't seem to have time or energy left to expend on such pagan "dogs" as the distraught woman who was so desperately pleading her case before him. After what seems like an initial attempt to duck the whole confrontation, he tells her so.

Compelled by her daughter's desperate need, the woman won't take "no" for an answer. In a masterful example of debating skill, she ignores the insult and turns Jesus' logic against him. "Lord," she says, "even the dogs eat the crumbs that fall from the table of their masters' table." And then Jesus changes his mind. Now he really sees this woman for who she is—not a person distant from God but one who is able to see the divine presence in him clearly, more so, perhaps, than he does himself! Now the miraculous transformation flows effortlessly through Jesus and into the woman's life.

A Model for the Church

Some years ago I wrote a reflection on this story for *U.S. Catholic* magazine. In response, a friend made an interesting observation: wouldn't it be something, he wrote, if this story could serve as a model for the Church? Just as Jesus himself could change his mind on fundamental issues when the needs of the people demanded it, so could the Church. His letter made me think: could this be the reason this gospel story was preserved in the first place?

One of the many insights into the development of the New Testament brought to light by Bible scholars in the past century (and incorporated into mainstream Catholic teaching through the Vatican Council II) is that the gospels are not biographies, as we know them today, of Jesus of Nazareth. (I will review the process of development in more detail in Chapter One). Over the course of several generations following Jesus' crucifixion and resurrection, the first Christians preserved stories about Jesus' miraculous healings and memories of his teachings through the process of oral tradition. During this time, these stories were edited and reshaped to serve the particular needs of various Christian communities.

When the gospel writers began their work, they once again edited the material available to them and selected only some of the rich traditions about Jesus that existed. The author of John's gospel tells us this explicitly: "Now Jesus did many other signs in the presence of his disciples, which are not written in this book. But these are written so that you may come to believe that Jesus is the Messiah, the Son of God, and that through believing you may have life in his name" (John 20:30–31).

But back to that gospel story: with so much to choose from, and with the stated intention of fostering belief in Jesus, why would any of the evangelists include a story that highlights Jesus' reluctance to work a miracle? The answer to this question, and the basic premise for this book, is that from the beginning Christians have understood that the image of the Holy Spirit as "wind and fire" during that first Pentecost (Acts 2), conveys a profound truth. Just as fire and wind are powerful and unpredictable, so is God.

As the first Jewish disciples of the risen Christ struggled to reinterpret their traditional beliefs about how the Messiah would reveal himself, the community gradually came to understand much more deeply how incomprehensibly different God's ways can be than our ways. To remain faithful as a community, these first Christians and all of their spiritual descendants would have to let go of everything at a moment's notice if discipleship required it—even preconceived notions of how God ought to act and what the Church ought to look like. Just as Jesus himself redefined his mission in the light of real circumstances—the need of the Canaanite women—the Church too must continually redefine itself.

The Obstacle of Fundamentalism

Again and again, two types of fundamentalism try to drive a wedge between the Christian community and the Holy Spirit, crippling our ability to be disciples of Christ. The first is biblical fundamentalism, which takes an overly simplistic view of the Bible as a single literary work almost untouched by human hands and written by a single author—God. It rejects a deeper understanding of the books of the Bible as the result of a complex process of development that took place over centuries. This type of fundamentalism has been unambiguously and consistently rejected by the Catholic Church in modern as well as ancient times.

The second kind of fundamentalism, however, has been much more bedeviling for Catholics. Just as biblical fundamentalism takes an overly simplistic view of the Bible, "ecclesial" fundamentalism takes an overly simplistic view of the Church. More specifically, it tends to distort the meaning of apostolic succession. This is the belief that the "deposit of faith" containing essential Christian teaching on faith and morals has been handed down in an unbroken line starting with the twelve apostles and continuing through their successors, the bishops and the popes.

Ecclesial fundamentalism sees this process of apostolic succession as taking place in a hermetically sealed vacuum. Nothing can get in or out. Even when the presentation of doctrine in one era contradicts the presentation of doctrine in another, ecclesial fundamentalists ignore or disclaim this. And the idea that the Holy Spirit might also be speaking through those not in ordained ministry, incorporated in the term *sensus fidelium* (sense of the faithful) is dismissed as heresy.

This kind of fundamentalist thinking is vividly illustrated in a notorious quote attributed to Pope Pius IX, whose papacy encompassed a good part of the nineteenth century. When the pope was questioned by an advisor who felt a particular pronouncement of his might not be consistent with tradition, Pius angrily responded, "I am tradition!" In reality, the Church has been challenged time and time again throughout its history to reinvent itself in order to remain faithful to the mission entrusted to it by Jesus.

Sometimes changes have come from the "bottom up," as when the faithful arrive where the Holy Spirit is leading long before the magisterium realizes it's time to pack. Other times have been from the "top down" as the pope and bishops must lead the community into extremely unpopular terrain or must set boundaries beyond which true Christian communion would be impossible. Most often change occurs as a result of "the dance." The Holy Spirit gently but profoundly moves both the faithful and the magisterium in prayerful—and sometimes not so prayerful—discernment in order to bring to light that fuller understanding of the Christian faith or *sensus fidei* (distinct from the *sensus fidelium*). Church history is a dynamic and often messy process through which the Holy Spirit is calling the body of Christ to change. Understanding and accepting this is the only sure antidote to ecclesial fundamentalism.

This process of constantly discerning what is Tradition and thus from God and what is merely changeable human custom has been going on within the Church since the beginning. In this book, we'll simplify things by focusing on eight dramatic turning points through which former ways of being Church gave way to new models. Often these changes were made to address new needs in changing times. Sometimes they were thrust upon the Church by history. In some cases the transformation can be seen clearly. In other cases it remains a struggle to understand the implications.

The purpose of this book is to help you see what you already know in your heart and have experienced in your own life. We are all a bit like the man who had five theories about raising children and then quickly became the man with five children and no theories! Change is inevitable and some theories drop away with change as others develop with change. Jesus calls us to courageously follow him, but he rarely passes out roadmaps. When we walk together, caught up in the Spirit, and not in our preconceived notions about what it means to be Church, we always find our way, two thousand years and counting.

Part One

The Early Church

ONE

The Council of Jerusalem

One of the most difficult concepts for my high school students is that the first "Christians" weren't Christian. They were Jews. Jesus was a Jew. All of the disciples of Jesus mentioned by name in the gospels are Jews. The first written proclamation of the *kerygma*, the core of the good news about Jesus, begins by stating, "Christ died for our sins in accordance with the Scriptures" (1 Corinthians 15:3). Jesus is identified as "Christ," the Greek translation of the Hebrew "messiah," and the Scriptures being referred to are the books of the Hebrew Scriptures (Old Testament).

The disciples of Jesus saw him as the Messiah long promised to Israel by God. Though a messiah "rising from the dead" was not what they expected, the first Christians saw themselves as Jews and understood their new faith through traditional Jewish beliefs and concepts. In the Acts of the Apostles, which is the only written account we have of the activities of this first generation of Christians, we learn that even after the Pentecost event this first generation of the Church continued to go up to the temple to pray (see Acts 3:1, for example).

Enter Saint Paul

All of this changed with the conversion of Saul of Tarsus. Better known to us as Paul, this great Christian missionary to the Gentile (non-Jewish) world, redefined the Christian message so that non-Jews could be baptized as disciples of Christ. A close look at Paul's conversion experience and ministry reveals that this "revolution" was not really planned by Paul. When we first meet Saul of Tarsus, he is persecuting an unusual group of Jews who refer to their movement not as Christianity but as "the Way" (Acts 7:58; 8:1–4). Saul is a Pharisee (Acts 26:4–5), a fervent student of the Jewish Torah, and he is well versed in all of the particulars of Jewish ritual that are derived from the Torah.

Saul's religious fervor also extended to worshiping God in the temple in Jerusalem as often as he could. He believed, as most Jews did at that time, that through the rituals performed at the temple, the people of Israel had special access to God. Pharisees like Paul differed sharply with the Sadducees, the Jewish priests who ran the temple complex and performed the rituals of sacrifice. Yet both groups understood that both temple worship and study of the Torah were necessary.

The followers of the Way, however, added another element. They were suggesting that a direct encounter with God was possible through a relationship with the risen Christ. Saul saw in this belief a serious threat to the two great pillars of the Jewish religion. "Breathing murderous threats," Saul headed off to Damascus with the authority to arrest any disciples of Jesus he might find there. The Acts of the Apostles portrays what happened next in a dramatic narrative:

> Now as he was going along and approaching Damascus, suddenly a light from heaven flashed around him. He fell to the ground and heard a voice saying to him, "Saul, Saul, why do you persecute me?" He asked, "Who are you, Lord?" The reply came, "I am Jesus, whom you are persecuting. But get up and enter the city, and you will be told what you are to do." (9:3–6)

The rest is history. Temporarily blinded, Saul of Tarsus was led into Damascus by his traveling companions. Three days later he was baptized by Ananias, a Christian disciple in Damascus, and "something like scales fell from his eyes, and his sight was restored" (Acts 9:18). After a period of discernment and introduction to some of the leaders of the Christian communities in Jerusalem and Antioch, Saul began the first of his missionary travels. In the rest of Acts, he will be referred to by his Roman name, Paul, signifying his ultimate destiny as apostle to the Gentiles.

History Revisted

Paul's destiny was not immediately clear, however. It unfolded gradually and not entirely as it is described in Acts. The Acts of the Apostles is not a primary "historical" source, so we need to look at the process through which the book was created. Acts is actually part of a two-volume work that also includes the Gospel of Luke. It was completed sometime in the late 80s or possibly early 90s of the first century AD. This means that Paul had been dead for about a generation (Church tradition holds Paul died around 64 AD) and his legacy within the Church had been firmly established before Luke told the story.

The story that Luke does tell is of an irresistible enterprise. Rooted in the Jewish faith, fully revealed in the person of Jesus of Nazareth, and brought to the Gentile world under the guidance of the Holy Spirit after the Resurrection, Christianity takes the Roman Empire by storm. Even the most fervent attempts to stop it by temple authorities and Roman governors prove futile. From the time of Paul's conversion, Luke makes it clear that his ultimate success is inevitable; he is God's special "instrument" (Acts 9:15). This is a perspective that would only have been possible in the later part of the first century, and certainly not during the early days of Paul's ministry. It is much more likely that Paul himself understood his mission after his conversion to be to his Jewish brothers and sisters. Given Paul's zealousness for his Jewish faith, it would be inevitable that once he was convinced Jesus was the messiah Israel anticipated, he would enthusiastically preach this good news throughout the synagogues of the Eastern Roman Empire.

And that's exactly what he did. The next time we see Paul after his conversion he is preaching in the synagogues of Damascus. During his first missionary journey with Barnabas and other traveling companions the pattern is always the same: they head for the local synagogue (see Acts 13:4, for example). Probably the best way to understand Paul's conversion experience is that Paul's personal encounter with the risen Jesus on the road to Damascus convinces him that the fulfillment of all of God's promises to Israel can be found in the risen Christ. In other words, Paul believes his Jewish faith is *fulfilled* through Jesus in whom temple and Torah are united and transcended.

Not many Jews buy Paul's message. He suffers under two enormous disadvantages that he simply cannot overcome. One, especially in the regions of Syria and Palestine, is a deep anger of the Jews who see him as a traitor. Paul was their champion of orthodoxy and now he is a spokesman for the very heresy he was entrusted to root out! But an even more intransigent problem is a messiah who saves through dying and rising, something most Jews found difficult to accept.

Suffering

The idea of a Messiah who liberates through suffering simply doesn't exist in the Old Testament. This sounds surprising to the modern Christian reader. Wasn't everything that Jesus does and says in accordance with the prophets? Wasn't everything that happened to Jesus during his Passion foretold?

Well, that depends on how you look at it. Certainly the Christian authors of the gospels believed this was so, as did their church communities, as do we. For about two generations before the gospels were written, memories of Jesus' words and deeds were preserved and connected with particular prophecies of the Old Testament. (I cover this process in more detail in my first book, *Unlocking the Treasures of the Bible.*) Even the way the stories were told reflect the Christian conviction that the Old Testament points to and is fulfilled in the New Testament. Compare, for example the way that Matthew portrays the circumstances surrounding the birth of Jesus (Matthew 1:2) with the story of Moses' birth recounted in Exodus (Exodus 1:2). For another example, see how Psalm 22 functions as a basic outline for the crucifixion account portrayed in the Gospel of Mark (Mark 15).

As Church tradition has always maintained, however, this Christian insight is only possible in the light of the Resurrection experience. Yet according to the Christian Scriptures themselves, this is an experience most Jews did not have. The most generous estimate of those who met the risen Christ in person, given by Paul in his first letter to the Corinthians, amounts to little more than 500 people (1 Corinthians 15:3–8). That number would've represented a minute proportion of the population of Galilee and Judea, the two principle Jewish population centers in Palestine.

When you look at the Old Testament prophecies without a Christian filter, the messianic oracles of such prophets as Ezekiel, Jeremiah, Isaiah, and Zechariah make no mention of the need for the Messiah to suffer. (See Isaiah 11:1–9 or Zechariah 9:9–17, for example.) The well-known "Servant of the Lord" songs in the book of Isaiah (42:1–4; 49:1–7; 50:4–11; 52:13–53) paint a picture of innocent suffering and are often quoted in the Passion account of the New Testament. There is no indication, however, that these oracles were originally intended as *messianic* prophesies. It's not surprising, therefore, that with a few notable exceptions, such as Priscilla and Aquila (Acts 18), Paul's ministry to his Jewish sisters and brothers soon reached a dead end.

Here Comes Everybody
During the course of Paul and Barnabas's first journey, however, something unexpected begins to happen. As the two men and their traveling companions make their way through Cyprus and southern Asia Minor, they begin to attract the attention of some Gentiles. Studies of Church history have revealed that the roots of Christianity as we know it extend into the cities of the Eastern Roman Empire. More specifically, while early church communities likely included a few wealthy patrons, Christianity's appeal was mostly to the masses of urban poor. (Notice how Luke, who is writing for a Church with a large Gentile population, emphasizes the poverty and simplicity of Jesus' birth in a way that Matthew never does; compare Luke 2 with Matthew 1—2.)

There are two main reasons for this unexpected turn of events. Religion in the Roman Empire has been compared to a carnival: numerous gods and goddesses were competing for the attention of the devout. Exotic cults from Egypt and points East came into the empire through conquest and trade. And among specific groups within the empire, such as the wealthy or the military, particular mystery cults that included secret ceremonies and rights of passage were popular. Although the Romans were coldly efficient and often brutal in governing the peoples they conquered, they were extremely tolerant of the rich stew of religions being practiced. Learning about a new religion being preached in town, therefore, offered an opportunity for at least entertainment and perhaps knowledge and insight.

More importantly, Jesus' message promised liberation from the oppression that was characteristic of the lives of the poor. Even today the most fervent Christians are in some of the poorest areas of the world. The Gentiles had no preconceived notions or interest in the Jewish idea of a messiah, or any of the particulars of Jewish laws; they offered Paul and Barnabas a clean slate upon which they could develop their teachings about the risen Christ.

There's a wonderfully dramatic story in Acts that gives us a window into how the ministry to the Gentiles might have unfolded. Paul and Barnabas arrive at Lystra in Asia Minor, and in the course of their preaching they encounter a man who has been crippled and lame from birth. Just as the power of the Holy Spirit was made manifest through Jesus in Luke's gospel, now that same power flows through the apostles in Acts. Paul commands the man to stand up straight and immediately he does. As soon as he realizes what has happened to him, the man begins to shout and jump around attracting a large crowd. Chaos erupts as the crowd makes preparations to offer a sacrifice of thanksgiving in the main temple in the town square. The reason? The townspeople are convinced that Paul and Barnabas are gods who have come to bestow special blessings on their town.

Paul and Barnabas determinedly try to correct this misunderstanding. Finally they succeed, but just barely. No sooner have things begun to calm down when a group from the local synagogue arrives and is able to rile up the crowd once again—this time *against* Paul and Barnabas. Paul barely escapes with his life (Acts 14:8–19). Despite all the insanity, some seeds are planted: "When they arrived, they called the Church together and related all that God had done with them, and how he had opened a door of faith for the Gentiles" (Acts 14:27).

Two Factions Develop

News of Paul and Barnabas' successes among the Gentiles filters south from Antioch in Syria to Jerusalem. Within the Jerusalem Church two factions begin to develop. Those who originally come from the Greek-speaking regions of the Eastern Roman Empire—the Hellenists—are used to interacting with Gentiles and with their customs. Temple worship and strict observance of the Torah have never been essential parts of their Judaism.

not believe in resurrection

Others, however, are not so open. The church in Jerusalem consisted in part of Pharisees and Sadducees who had become followers of the way. For this group and the like-minded—known as "the Judaizers"—following the requirements of the Torah and worshiping at the temple were non-negotiable parts of being a follower of Jesus. After all, wasn't Jesus himself a devout Jew? (Jesus says as much in the beginning of the Sermon on the Mount.) In the eyes of these early Christians, being a disciple of Jesus meant being a good Jew. If the Gentiles wanted to be in communion, they would first have to accept the teachings of Judaism, starting with circumcision! (Try and imagine how well this went over in the Gentile world.)

But Paul saw things differently. If the risen Christ is the source of our salvation, Paul reasoned, then the Torah and the temple are not. While certainly both were important to Paul, a Pharisee himself, neither seemed essential any longer. He puts it this way in his letter to the Galatians:

> Now before faith came, we were imprisoned and guarded under the law until faith would be revealed. Therefore the law was our disciplinarian until Christ came, so that we might be justified by faith. But now that faith has come, we are no longer subject to a disciplinarian, for in Christ Jesus you are all children of God through faith. As many of you as were baptized into Christ have clothed yourselves with Christ. (Galatians 3:23–27)

council Jerusalem

Either Christ's gift is unconditional or it isn't, Paul reasoned. Something had to give. Was it absolutely necessary to require Gentiles to become Jews as the Judaizers insisted? Or should the Church adopt a more open-door policy toward Gentiles who wished to become disciples of Jesus? Somewhere in the mid-40s of the first century, a gathering took place in Jerusalem aimed at settling the question once and for all. That meeting is referred to today as the Council of Jerusalem. *40 od*

certainly not have to become

The Council Meets *of Jerusalem 40 AP Jews*

The New Testament contains two accounts of this meeting in Jerusalem. One is found in Paul's letter to the Galatians written five to ten years after the meeting. The other is the story told in Acts 14, probably written forty or fifty years after the meeting. Not surprisingly, Luke tidies things up a bit in Acts. Once the council's decision is put into a formal letter signed by the leader of the Jerusalem Church, James, "the brother of the Lord," the controversy never comes up again. Paul's earlier account suggests the process was more complicated. His confrontation with Peter described in Galatians 2 is prompted by the presence of Judaizers in Antioch *after* the council has reached its decision.

Allowing for these differences, the basic accounts are the same. Paul and Barnabas travel to Jerusalem to meet with Peter, James, and "the apostles and the elders" (Acts 15:6). Probably in an example of revisionist history, Peter's waffling over the issue (suggested by Paul in Galatians) is gone. Instead, it is Peter who speaks on Paul's behalf, emphatically stating his belief that the Holy Spirit "in cleansing [the Gentiles'] hearts by faith he has made no distinction between them and us....We believe that we will be saved through the grace of the Lord Jesus, just as they will"(Acts 15:9–11).

The assembly sits in silence as Paul and Barnabas get up to speak next and tell the Jerusalem leaders about "the signs and wonders that God had done through them among the Gentiles." Finally, James settles the issue, announcing in the conclusion of his speech the policy that has governed the Church ever since: "Therefore I have reached the decision that we should not trouble those Gentiles who are turning to God" (Acts 15:12–19).

The Jerusalem leaders do impose a few minor conditions concerning the laws of ritual purity and the dietary laws of Judaism, but the decision is clear. Gentiles do not have to become Jews in order to be disciples of Jesus. In extending the hand of community beyond the boundaries of its Jewish incubator, the Church took an enormous step toward becoming truly catholic, that is, universal. Having resolved the controversy to his satisfaction, Paul would spend the rest of his life on the road, traveling through Asia Minor, Greece, and eventually finding his way to Rome, leaving a number of new, mostly Gentile, churches in his wake.

And so the Church changed its mind. Challenged by the unanticipated success of the Gentile mission, the first Jewish followers of the Way were forced to prayerfully look more deeply at their understanding of Jesus and of themselves. Over the course of the next generation after the council, these first disciples and their successors gradually came to see themselves as pioneers in a new way of being in communion with God. Then in 70 AD, a calamity befell Jerusalem that moved the Church irrevocably into the Gentile world.

The Destruction of the Temple *70 AD, Roman occupation*

Relations between the Jews in Palestine and their Roman occupiers had never been good. Soon after the Romans under Pompey were "invited" to enter the Jewish lands in 64 BC, the Jews began to feel the weight of Roman rule and taxation. One hundred years later, the occupation had become almost intolerable for most Jews. There had almost been a revolution a few years after Jesus' crucifixion when Emperor Gaius (Caligula) planned on placing a statue of himself in the sacred precincts of the Jerusalem temple. Fortunately, the Emperor died before the plan could be carried out.

No occupation is ever really welcomed by the people who have been conquered. The Roman occupation in Judea was particularly bitter for two specific reasons, however. For one thing, Jerusalem and the surrounding territories were located near the eastern frontier of the empire. Every major town was equipped with a garrison of soldiers whose job was to be on the lookout for threats from the Parthians to the East or internal rebellion by Jewish zealots. (Notice how often Roman soldiers are on the periphery—and sometimes in the center—of gospel stories.) Jesus' crucifixion was probably typical of the way the Romans handled real or potential rebel movements. Surviving records suggest that hundreds or even thousands of Jews were crucified during the Roman occupation.

A second source of conflict was the unusual nature of the Jewish religion. Virtually all of the peoples in the Roman Empire worshiped multiple gods and goddesses. As a result, they had no real problem with performing public acts of sacrifice on behalf of the Roman emperor. The Jews, however, believed in only one God, and the first commandment clearly prohibited them from worshiping idols. Throughout the entire time of Rome's control, Jews fervently resisted any attempts to institute a cult of emperor worship in Palestine, and this led to many violent confrontations between Jews and Roman soldiers. (See Acts 5:35–37 for examples of conflict.) At least one massacre took place during the governorship of Pontius Pilate. You will even find the name of a zealot (a guerrilla fighter of the Jewish resistance) in the list of Jesus' twelve apostles (Luke 6:15).

In part, the conspiracy to eliminate Jesus was motivated by a desire to put off the day of the final confrontation between the Jews and the Romans, a battle the Jews had no practical hopes of winning. The inevitable became reality in 66 AD when, provoked by the last Roman procurator of Judea, the inhabitants rose up in revolt. By the time Rome had crushed the insurrection four years later, the city of Jerusalem, including the temple complex, lay in ruins.

Regrouping of the Jews

In the wake of this failed revolt, Judaism was reeling. For the next generation, the focus of Judaism shifted more and more toward strict observance of the Torah and showed less and less toleration for "fringe" sects that might complete the dissolution of the faith that the Roman army had started. The final divorce between Christianity and Judaism came in 100 AD at a meeting of the Jewish Pharisees at Jamnia, a coastal town in northern Palestine.

From the Jewish point of view, the now explicit Christian belief in the divinity of Jesus seemed to be a blatant violation of the first commandment. Following the meeting in Jamnia, Jews were pressured to choose: either leave the Way or leave the synagogue. Jewish communities all over the Eastern Roman Empire must have been torn asunder as families and individuals within families made their choices. The resulting hurt and anger against the Jews is frequently mentioned in the Gospel of John, which was written during this period. Of the four evangelists, only John consistently and with vehemence refers to the enemies of Jesus as "the Jews."

Estranged Siblings

As the second century began, the destiny of the Church as a Gentile community was sealed. One by one, Jewish-Christian communities were either absorbed into larger congregations (John's gospel shows some evidence of this) or disappeared as their numbers dwindled. Christianity and modern rabbinical Judaism went their separate ways. It is one of the darker chapters of Christian history that the relationship of these two "siblings," grounded in a misunderstanding of John's gospel and of the

Jewish faith in general, has too often resembled the relationship of Cain and Abel—with the Christian Church in the role of the persecuting Cain.

In modern times, however, things have been changing for the better. When we discuss the reforms of the Second Vatican Council, we will look at the process through which the Church began to understand and take the first halting steps to purge herself of anti-Semitism. Perhaps another turning point is just ahead, a time when the two people of the one covenant will stand together in harmony and see themselves as the children of Abraham and sisters and brothers of one another and of Jesus.

For Thought and Discussion

1) Read about Paul's conversion in Acts 9. Compare it to the disciples' encounter with the risen Christ on the road to Emmaus (Luke 24:13–35). How are the encounters similar and different? What insights do you gain from them into the Resurrection experience?

2) Reflect on your own conversion experience(s). When have you "seen the light"? How has this affected your life?

3) Paul's challenge was to communicate the essentials of discipleship to both Gentiles and Jews. Who are the people and groups who are communicating the essentials of Christian discipleship today? How are they doing it? What are the "essentials"?

4) Why was Paul's mission to the Jews a limited success? Why do you think he was more successful with the Gentiles?

5) Paul is sometimes referred to as the true founder of Christianity. Do you agree or disagree with this assessment? Why?

6) How does this period in Church history illustrate the Holy Spirit's shaping of the *sensus fidei* through the interaction of the magisterium and the faithful?

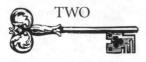

TWO

The Apostate Crisis

public deny Faith under threat + persecution

> *"Father, forgive them, for they know not what they do."*
>
> (Lk 23:34)

Luke's portrait of the dying Jesus pleading on behalf of his mocking tormentors has led countless numbers of Christians through the centuries into profound meditation on the nature of unconditional love and forgiveness. Time and time again in our history, we have been challenged individually and communally to forgive those who have done things we feel in our hearts to be unforgivable. And the hardest acts of forgiveness are often those directed toward loved ones who have betrayed us.

The martyrs certainly had much to forgive. Yet we imagine them singing psalms of joy as they were thrown into the Coliseum to be torn apart by wild animals. The Roman persecutions of the second to fourth centuries produced many martyrs, people of great courage who bravely and serenely accepted their fate, satisfying the incessant blood lust of the Roman citizenry. There is the story of Ignatius, the bishop of Antioch, who writes of his eagerness "to be ground fine by the teeth of lions so that I become the purest bread for Christ." The *Diary of Perpetua* and related writings portray the conversion, imprisonment, and dramatic execution of a young Roman noblewoman and her servant. "The blood of the martyrs," Tertullian wrote, "is the seed of the Church."

The Rest of the Story

A more objective analysis of the first three hundred years of Christian history gives us a different picture. Certainly those who went to their deaths for their faith did so nobly and bravely. The number of martyrs in proportion to the total number of Christians in the Roman empire, however, is small. For many decades after the resurrection of Jesus and the Pentecost experience, Christianity remained a small, mostly urban movement that for the most part escaped the notice of the authorities. Persecutions were sporadic, short-lived, and usually local. At any given time, the threat of actual persecution for most Christians was remote.

Three incidents in particular give us some sense of how the persecutions were conducted. The first recorded persecution of Christians is that of Emperor Nero in the mid-60s of the first century. Church tradition has long maintained that both Peter and Paul met their deaths during that persecution, Paul, the story goes, by beheading, and Peter by being crucified upside down. The persecution was small but brutal. The Roman historian Tacitus writes of Christians being rounded up and executed. Some were even used as human torches during Emperor Nero's garden party!

As horrible as these events were, they were not planned by Roman authorities to eliminate Christians. Suspicions were high that Nero had orchestrated the great fire that had destroyed much of Rome so that he could rebuild Rome. In search of a scapegoat to deflect that suspicion, Nero saw in the tiny Christian community of Rome the perfect candidate. Although the Council of Jerusalem had set the course for the eventual separation of Judaism and Christianity, as discussed in the previous chapter, the perception that Christians were an unusual sect of Judaism would endure for another century. Jews were never well liked by the Romans because of their stubborn refusal to worship the emperor. Given the fact that the Jewish war would begin only a few years after Nero's persecution, it is safe to assume that Jewish-Roman relations were at a low point.

And yet it must have appeared to Nero that, even within the Jewish community in Rome, these Christians (followers of a man called

"Chrestus," according to one ancient Roman source) were viewed with disdain. Nero took advantage of a perfect storm. All he needed to do was to spread a few rumors, send out misinformation, make a public example out of a few of the accused, and people would move on to the next crisis. Nero's plan was only partially successful, however; the sadistic means by which he executed the accused Christians sickened many in Rome and bore witness to his growing madness. Not long after this persecution, sensing that his days were numbered, Nero committed suicide.

Domitian's Persecution

The next report of Christian persecution after the death of Nero shows up during the reign of Emperor Domitian (81–96 AD). Information about this is slim, suggesting that once again the persecution was local to Rome. There may have been small outbreaks in North Africa and Asia Minor as well. (Accounts that do exist are not even entirely clear that it was Christians who were targeted. Dio Cassius merely states that those arrested had "slipped into Jewish customs.")

Our primary source of Domitian's persecution is an indirect one. A consensus of Catholic Bible scholars holds that the persecution of Domitian is the background for much of the symbolism and imagery in the book of Revelation. Disguised behind apocalyptic images are references, that when properly interpreted, fit well with what is known about the life and times of the late first century. One well-known example of such symbols is the infamous "666," the "mark of the beast" who is destined to appear as the final battle between good and evil begins (see Revelation 13).

Many books have been written at least in part attempting to crack the meaning of this number. The most likely explanation is that when the numbers are converted to their equivalent letter designations in Greek, the language of the book of Revelation, they make reference to Emperor Nero. (As is also true with Latin, the Greek language uses the same characters for numerals and letters.) There was an enduring belief, rooted in the terrible memories of Nero's reign, that he would one day return to wreak more havoc. In the eyes of the first Christians, particularly those still alive who would have remembered Nero's persecution, it must have seemed that in Domitian the prediction had been fulfilled with a vengeance.

The "Christian" Problem

What both of these early persecutions have in common, of course, is that they were largely confined to Rome. The first solid reference to conflicts between Christians and the Roman authorities outside of the capital is in a letter written by Pliny the Younger, the governor of the province of Bithynia in Asia Minor, to the Emperor Trajan in 112 AD. Pliny has a problem: having just arrived at his new post, he doesn't quite know what to do when individuals are brought before him on the charge of being Christian. (Technically, the charge would have been atheism, because Christians refused to acknowledge the existence of the Roman gods and goddesses!) In his first encounter with the group, he gave them several opportunities to make sacrifice to the Roman deities and to deny the charges against them. Those who did as instructed, he released; those who didn't, he executed. It's clear from his letter that Pliny himself has no certain idea of what Christians are or for what beliefs they stand. "Their obstinacy alone," he felt, was grounds for punishment.

Being a basically fair-minded man, he thought it appropriate to seek the emperor's opinion concerning his actions. Emperor Trajan's response gives us a sense of how small a phenomenon Christianity still was at the beginning of the second century. The emperor approves of Pliny's actions, but counsels him not to actively seek out the Christians. If any are accused before him, he advised, Pliny should continue to give them the opportunity to publicly deny their faith, and if they do so, let them go. While Christianity might be a nuisance, Trajan did not seem to think it posed any great threat to the Empire as a whole. Within a generation or so after the deaths of Pliny and Trajan, however, this benign neglect will begin to take a much darker turn.

Why the Christians Stood Out

While the Romans were coldly and sometimes brutally efficient at administering and defending their empire, they were notably tolerant toward the religions practiced by the peoples they conquered. This seemed like a certain way to maintain the peace and prosperity of the empire. Let the people worship as many gods and goddesses as they like. The only requirement the Romans did make was that everyone in the empire perform certain sacrifices to the gods on behalf of the emperor, something roughly equivalent to flying the flag on the fourth of July or standing and singing "The Star Spangled Banner" at the beginning of a baseball game.

For most, this was easy enough. But not for the Jews and Christians! For those who believed in only one God, there was no compromise. By the middle of the second century, Rome had been struggling for over two hundred years with what seemed to the empire to be a particular obstinacy among the Jews. Countless skirmishes had taken place in Judea culminating in violent wars in 66–70 AD and again in 135 AD which destroyed Jerusalem and ravaged surrounding areas.

Eventually, the Romans and Jews reached a certain uneasy truce. Jews were exempt from public rituals of sacrifice and from serving in the Roman military. While Judaism was a bizarre religion from the Roman point of view, no one could dispute its ancient roots, and that was something the Romans respected. Besides, the relative numbers of Jews in any given province in the empire was always small. They could easily be rounded up and exterminated if necessary. (This is a brutal reality that has plagued Jewish communities throughout the centuries, with the Holocaust as the most horrific example.)

For a time the Jewish exemption covered Christians as well. As the second century progressed and the Christian communities came more and more to be perceived as separate entities from Judaism, however, things changed. Although Christians were as stubborn as Jews in insisting on the worship of only one God, they did not have the ancient lineage of the Jews to fall back on. From the Roman point of view, Christianity was more of a superstition than a religion. What good could come of a movement that had its origin in the life and death of a crucified criminal? Even more unsettling to the Roman authorities, the Christian communities were growing. In some parts of the empire, they were already the majority.

Much of what citizens and subjects of the empire knew about Christianity in the second and third centuries was based on half-truths and rumors. Christians were accused of cannibalism because they "ate flesh" and "drank blood." Their incessant talk about loving their brothers and sisters led to accusations of incest. Most disturbing of all, however, was their unabashed pride in their refusal to worship the Roman deities. How long would the gods and goddesses allow such insults to go unpunished? What effect would such blatant blasphemy have on the empire as a whole?

Local Atrocities

By the middle of the second century, persecutions, although still local, were becoming more organized and more intense. Between 165 and 168, a persecution broke out in the province of Smyrna in Asia Minor. Rather than just rounding up Christians at random, however, local officials also arrested the aged Polycarp, the bishop of the church residing in that region. The dramatic account of Polycarp's refusal to deny the faith and ultimate martyrdom is preserved in an early history of the Church written by Eusebius of Caesarea. About a decade later, an even fiercer persecution broke out in what is now the French city of Lyon. The surviving account of that event, again related by Eusebius, suggests that this persecution was intensified by mob violence.

One of the most dramatic stories from this time is an account of a persecution that broke out in the city of Carthage, North Africa, in the beginning of the third century. According to the account, a young Roman noblewoman named Perpetua was preparing to become a Christian and was arrested along with other members of the catechumenate (those preparing to become Christians). A short time after Perpetua gave birth to the child she was carrying, she was marched off to the local arena along with her servant Felicitas and some others. When the wild beasts unleashed in the arena failed to do their job, a Roman soldier was sent into the arena to slit the throats of the two women. The young soldier's hand trembled so much that he was unable to complete the deed until Perpetua held his hand and helped him find his mark. This story and many others are contained in *Acts of the Martyrs*, a mixture of fact and legend.

Empire-wide Persecution

The years between the death of Emperor Marcus Aurelius in 180 AD and the ascension of Decius to the throne in 249 were years of trouble for the empire. Beginning with Marcus Aurelius's son Commodus, the majority of the emperors in this period were either tyrants or incompetents. Assassinations were common. Not coincidently, the empire experienced increasing pressures from Germanic tribes who began to breach the borders of the empire and invade the cities. When the Roman general Decius gained the throne he wasted no time in taking decisive steps to stem the chaos.

By this time Christianity was no longer a curiosity within the empire but a substantial presence—or threat—in the eyes of many Romans. It did not take a great leap of imagination for many to wonder if the empire's troubles and the ascendancy of Christianity were linked. Decius decided it was time to do something about this problem.

This persecution, however, was not local. Typical persecutions only moved Christians from one region of the empire to another. To eradicate Christianity once and for all would take an empire-wide effort. Decius issued a degree requiring all citizens and subjects of the empire to carry certificates (*libelli*) certifying that they had performed public acts of worship to the pagan deities. Anyone who could not produce the certificate was subject to arrest, imprisonment, and even execution. The emperor knew that Christians would face the choice of either publicly denying their faith or being arrested. Either way, the Christian communities would be decimated.

The persecution proceeded in two phases. Initial efforts were concentrated on rooting out the leaders of the local Christian Churches in an effort to demoralize and confuse the movement. Fabian, the bishop of Rome, was arrested, tried and executed in 250. Thousands of Christians throughout the Empire must have lived in terror as the persecution moved into a second phase. It's impossible to know what effect the persecution would have had on the very survival of the Church had Decius not been killed in battle in 251. Even so, the blow the emperor inflicted was a severe one. The aftermath of the persecution found the faithful deeply divided over an issue that threatened to complete the process Decius had begun.

The Apostate Crisis

The Church has always been a pilgrim church. Though animated by a divine presence, it is made up of human beings attempting to follow Jesus as best they can. Some live up to the challenge and some do not. Just so, not every Christian in the early centuries chose arrest and potential execution over public denial of their faith. Many Christians, including some Church leaders, did obtain the *libelli*. Such a certificate might have said something like this: "I have always sacrificed to the gods, and now in your presence in accordance with the edict, I have made sacrifice, and poured a libation" (W.H.C. Frend, *The Early Church*, p. 98).

Christians obtained these certificates through a variety of means and for a variety of reasons. Wealthy Christians were often able to purchase them through bribery. Others simply went through the motions, having made the decision that the lesser of the two evils between abandoning their families or communities and performing a meaningless sacrifice was to give the pagans what they wanted. Still others residing in cities such as Alexandria or Carthage where the persecution was particularly fierce sacrificed to the pagan gods out of sheer terror. Surely some sacrificed to the gods because their faith was lukewarm. Christians who publicly denied their faith, for whatever reason, were referred to as apostates. (The actual title given to this group in the aftermath of the Decian persecution were the *lapsi*, the lapsed.) These were the men and women who had turned their backs on the community and on Christ.

After Decius's death, the Church was divided to the core over two questions: 1) Were the sacraments valid when conferred by ministers who had sacrificed to the pagan gods? 2) Should apostates who sought readmission into the Church ever be allowed to resume their place in the community? The attempt to resolve these questions occupied much time and energy in the ensuing years.

Stephen and Cyprian

The story that played itself out in the church residing at Carthage, a major city in North Africa, gives us a good insight into the depth of this crisis and the eventual direction of its resolution. During the great persecution, the bishop of Carthage, Cyprian, was forced to go into hiding from the Roman authorities who were seeking his life. When he returned to Carthage after the persecution had abated, he found that, in his absence, local church leaders had begun to hand out "letters of peace" to the apostates, welcoming them back into the community unconditionally. It's likely that this decision was made partly out of a pastoral intent to restore peace and partly out of a desire to upstage their bishop. Cyprian was outraged at this apparent refusal to acknowl-

*Cyprian want permanent exclusion
of lapsed ministers sacrament not valid*

edge the terrible scandal caused to the faithful by the apostates' blatant acts of betrayal.

As soon as he was able, Cyprian called together a council of bishops at Carthage which rejected these letters of peace and insisted that those Christians who had actually sacrificed to the pagan gods could only be admitted to communion with the Church on their deathbeds. Those who had obtained *libelli* through bribery or other means, but had not actually sacrificed, might be readmitted after having successfully satisfied a panel of inquiry and performing significant public penances. Presumably based on the logic that those with greater responsibility must be held to a higher standard, Cyprian and the other bishops declared that any presbyter (roughly the equivalent of priest), deacon, elder, or bishop who had lapsed during the persecution was excommunicated permanently. Furthermore, any sacraments they had administered were not valid.

It took several years after the martyrdom of Fabian for a strong leader to emerge once again in Rome. Finally, that happened on May 12, 254, when Stephen was elected pope. Stephen was keenly aware of the division within the local churches. Rigorists such as Cyprian, and an even more extreme Roman theologian named Novatian, did not want to accommodate the apostates in general and wanted nothing to do with ordained ministers who had publicly denied the faith. The elders at Carthage who cared for the community in Cyprian's absence represented the other extreme: those who in their eagerness to restore unity to the Church wished to put the apostate crisis behind them as quickly as possible.

In considering what would be best for long-term Christian unity, Stephen and many others within the Church recognized the extreme nature of these solutions. Cyprian's stance would leave enormous numbers of the faithful excommunicated from the body of Christ. Even if they had not committed acts of apostasy themselves, they might have received the sacraments from ministers who were apostates.

Stephen was also of the belief that the grace of a sacrament was grounded in the sacrament itself and in the disposition of the recipient (*ex opere operato*), not in the good standing of the minister (*ex opere operantis*). The fundamental difference between the two men was the way in which they understood the nature of the Church. Stephen envisioned a Church that included a (developing) hierarchy and formal rituals through which the faithful could encounter God. It was an idea that Augustine would express clearly a century later in response to another controversy: "There are many whom the Catholic Church has that God does not have, and many that God has whom the Catholic Church does not have."

At the other extreme was an equal threat to Christian unity, however. As appealing as the position of the elders of the Carthaginian community was, Stephen recognized that it did not acknowledge the reality of sin and its consequences. To simply readmit the lapsed without requiring any kind of demonstration of their remorse would eliminate the process of healing and forgiveness. How can the community forgive those who have not repented? Allowing the lapsed to return as if nothing had happened was to deny the seriousness of the painful persecutions many had endured.

Battle of the Bishops

In an attempt to initiate healing and recovery Stephen counseled a middle course. He advised that as long as the sacraments were administered properly—for example, that baptism was performed using the proper Trinitarian formula—they should be viewed as valid even if the minister had lapsed into apostasy. Furthermore, any of the apostates who wished to be readmitted to the Church, whether they had performed public sacrifices or not, should be welcomed back into the local church community after performing an appropriate act of public penance. The exact nature of that penance would be left up to the local communities to determine.

Reactions were immediate and passionate. Some Spanish congregations pleaded with Cyprian for support in their position that sacraments performed by apostate bishops should remain invalid. Cyprian called together another council in Carthage in 256, through which he reaffirmed his earlier position. Stephen was criticized for his presumption in attempting to impose the Roman understanding of Church and sacraments on other communities. Many local churches in Asia Minor were sympathetic to Cyprian's position as well. We don't really know how Stephen responded to all of this; most of the correspondence that survives comes from Carthage. It appears that by the time of Stephen's death in 257, the two bishops had basically agreed to disagree.

Consider for a moment what this controversy between Stephen and Cyprian reveals about the nature of the Christian Church in these early centuries. Clearly Cyprian believes his decisions carry the same authority as those of Stephen, more so in his own Carthaginian community. A number of other local churches must have seen things the same way, judging by the Spaniards' decision to go over Stephen's head. Christianity in those seminal days was mostly a local affair, with each community tending to its own needs and concerns. Collectively these local churches saw themselves in union spiritually but not necessarily administratively or even doctrinally.

Gradually the churches in the larger cities of the empire, Carthage, Alexandria, and Antioch, for example, gained influence over local churches in the surrounding areas. The idea of one, holy, apostolic church, as we now understand it in the Roman Catholic tradition, was still centuries away. When Cyprian went to his own death as a martyr during a revival of the Decian persecution by a later emperor, he did so as a brother to the bishop of Rome but in no way subject to his decrees.

Yet at the same time, it would be incorrect to say that the bishop of Rome was simply one bishop among many. (The title pope or "papa" began as an informal term of affection among the people of Rome for their bishop.) His position as the successor to Peter did give that office a special prominence among the other communities that made up the body of Christ. While the Spaniards disapproved of Stephen's counsel, they also recognized the need to align themselves with another bishop of great prestige if they were going to oppose him. The very fact that Stephen's opinion was sought in the first place is further evidence of the important role the bishop of Rome played.

The basic position advanced by Stephen would gradually take hold. In the apostate crisis, the Church was compelled by circumstances to face several crucial questions. Did it truly believe the fundamental truth—revealed through the Incarnation—that the universe was grounded in unconditional love? That it was never more obviously the body of Jesus Christ than when it embraced the repentant sinner with enthusiastic and heartfelt joy? That God's plan of salvation was not the private possession of any group but intended for every human being who was created out of the loving essence of the Trinity? This was the proclamation Jesus Christ brought to the world, and it was through his body, the Church, that the revelation was unfolding.

Stephen's decision shows the magisterium of the Church at its best. The bishop of Rome gave words and prescribed actions which incorporated the promptings of the Holy Spirit within the consciences of the faithful, promptings that were blocked in the hearts of many by the pain and suffering caused by persecution.

In leading with the mercy of God over human concepts of justice, Stephen helped to point the Church in the right direction and helped those who would listen find their way toward their truest selves. His insistence that the sacraments of the Church are not dependent on those who administer them but on the grace that flows through them was a strong reaffirmation of the point Jesus made in overturning the tables of the moneychangers in the outer courtyard of the temple in Jerusalem. (See John 2:13–25, for example.) No one—and no institution, however sacrosanct—has a monopoly on God's love and forgiveness.

There are many reasons why the number of Christians in the latter half of the third century grew exponentially throughout the Roman empire, but certainly one of them was a growing awareness that these early Christian communities meant what they said. They were "catholic" (meaning universal) in the best sense, opening themselves up to all who would come, Jew and Greek, rich and poor, barbarian and Roman, sinner and saint. This emerging Catholicism was showing it could both hold fast to essential elements of the faith and change those elements which were not essential, in accordance with the movement of the Holy Spirit.

For Thought and Discussion

1) Read some of the entries in *Acts of the Martyrs*. (See the *New Catholic Encyclopedia* or the *Anchor Bible Dictionary* as a starting point.) Which stories touch you? Inspire you? Repulse you? Does it matter to you that in many of these stories it is difficult to separate historical facts from myths and legends? Why or why not?

2) Identify the following:
   - Perpetua and Felicitas
   - Pliny the Younger
   - Polycarp
   - Tertullian
   - Domitian
   - Cyprian
   - Decius
   - Stephen

   Who is the strongest model for you? Why?

3) What were some reasons that early Christians might have chosen to become apostates? How do you think the apostates seeking reinstatement ought to have been handled by their communities? Why?

4) Reflect on a time in your life when you felt the most pressure to publicly deny a cherished belief. What was the source of the pressure? What did you do? How do you feel about the situation now? What did you learn?

5) Read some accounts of the meetings among bishops at the gatherings of the United States Catholic Conference of Bishops. (Check out the website at www.usccb.org.) What are some controversial issues the bishops have discussed? How have they handled the controversies?

6) In your opinion, what is the difference between responsible dialogue within the Church and irresponsible dissent? How can we tell the difference?

7) Concerning the interplay between the magisterium and the *sensus fidelium*: how much influence should the community have on the decisions their bishops make? Why? Should we return to a system of popular election of bishops? Why or why not?

THREE

The End of an Era

On the day which is dedicated to the sun, all those who live in the cities or who dwell in the countryside gather in a common meeting, and for as long as there is time, the Memoirs of the Apostles or the writings of the prophets are read. Then, when the reader has finished, the president verbally gives a warning and appeal for the imitation of these good examples.

Then we all rise together and offer prayers, and, as we said before, when our prayer is ended, bread is brought forward along with wine and water, and the president likewise gives thanks to the best of his ability, and the people call out their assent, saying Amen. Then there is the distribution to each and the participation in the eucharistic elements, which also are sent with the deacons to those who are absent. Those who are wealthy and who wish to do so, contribute whatever they themselves care to give; and the collection is placed with the president, who aids the orphans and the widows, and those who through sickness or any other cause are in need, and those who are imprisoned, and the strangers who are sojourning with us—and, in short, he takes care of all who are in need.

It will come as no surprise to anyone that these two paragraphs contain a description of the celebration of the Eucharist, more commonly known as the Mass. What might be surprising, however, is that this description was written by Justin the Martyr somewhere around 150 AD! The liturgy we gather to celebrate today is essentially unchanged from that of our earliest ancestors in the faith. And yet something significant has changed. If you look more closely at that passage, you will also notice the absence of most of the formal ministries we take for granted today. Not a bishop or priest in sight! And while the term "deacon" is recognizable, his (or her) responsibilities are not to assist with the celebration of the liturgy but to go out into the community to serve the spiritual and material needs of its members. This is a celebration rooted in the community, celebrated by the members of the community in the presence of Jesus, and the needs of the sick, impoverished, and oppressed were firmly kept in mind.

The "president," the presider of the assembly, was not sent to the community by a distant bishop (after having spent years in an isolated formation program before entering into full-time ministry). In this early stage of Church history, the presider was a Christian who lived in the community and who had been chosen *by the faithful of that community* to lead the assembly in its weekly celebration. In most local churches, the office was a part-time position as would be the case with a permanent deacon in the Church today. This early Christian Church was truly a populist movement. The story of how that Church was transformed into an institution with a distinct and preeminent hierarchy—from a circle to a pyramid—is the third major turning point in our examination of Church history.

By the People, for the People

Beginning in apostolic times, Christianity was an enterprise of the laity. How could it be otherwise? Just look at the list of those at the epicenter of the ministry of Jesus of Nazareth. Four fishermen (Simon Peter, Andrew, James, and John) and a tax collector (Matthew) were among the Twelve. According to the Gospel of John, the first apostle to proclaim the Resurrection is a woman known as Mary of Magdala (John 20:11–18). With the notable exceptions of Saul of Tarsus, Joseph of Arimathea, and, again according to John, Nicodemus, there does

not seem to have been much of an interest in Jesus' ministry among
the Pharisees and Saduccees, the religious authorities of Jesus' day.
Often the charge leveled against Jesus by his opponents to discredit
him is that he eats and drinks with sinners, tax collectors, prostitutes,
all those, in other words, perceived by the elite to be on the marginal
side of society.

If there were any doubts at all about Jesus' commitment to the disenfranchised, they were dispelled by his dramatic cleansing of the temple, the memory of which is recounted in all four gospels. That may
very well have been the definitive act that hardened the opposition
against Jesus. Mark, Matthew, and Luke all suggest this by placing the
story within their Passion accounts.

The specifics of what Jesus did are well known, most dramatically
conveyed in John's account:

> The Passover of the Jews was near, and Jesus went up to
> Jerusalem. In the temple he found people selling cattle, sheep,
> and doves, and the money-changers seated at their tables.
> Making a whip of cords, he drove all of them out of the tem-
> ple, both the sheep and the cattle. He also poured out the
> coins of the money-changers and overturned their tables. He
> told those who were selling the doves, "Take these things out
> of here! Stop making my Father's house a market-place!"
> (John 2:13–16)

Why Did Jesus Do This?

What may not be so well known is why Jesus did what he did. In
ancient Judaism, temple worship was an essential part of Jewish life. All
Jews in Palestine were exhorted to make a pilgrimage to Jerusalem during the most important feasts in the Jewish calendar, including the
Passover. Various animal sacrifices were ritually prescribed to accom-
pany the prayers during the festivals. At Passover, for example, the male
head of the household would lead a lamb through the outer courtyards
of the temple complex toward the gate that marked the entrance to the
Court of the Priests. At that point a priest would take the animal into
the innermost courtyard of the temple complex and ritually slaughter
the animal on the Altar of Sacrifice.

Only the temple priests could perform the sacrifice. And the suppli-
cant could only purchase an animal for sacrifice from the merchants in
the outermost courtyard (the Court of the Gentiles), and had to pay for
it with a particular type of coin available from the moneychangers. The
normal Roman currency of the day was not allowed into the sacred
precincts of the temple because it contained graven images of the
emperor and of the Roman pagan gods and goddesses. The moneychangers would exchange the Roman coins with the appropriate
coinage, for a fee, of course.

To put it simply, by Jesus' time the temple complex had become a
vast financial monopoly benefiting the priests (Sadducees), their
administrative assistants, and the Roman authorities. In addition to the
inevitable price-gouging that is the product of any monopoly, the
whole corrupt system sent an awful message to the Jewish people. It
seemed that a direct relationship with God was possible for only a
select few whose hypocrisy was apparent. This scandalous attempt to
render God inaccessible was what Jesus so violently rejected.

Apostolic Equality

While specific accounts of the day-to-day life in the local churches during the first two centuries of Christian history is scarce, there is enough
evidence to conclude that the populist spirit of Jesus' ministry was
incarnated in the Church after his death and resurrection. In both the
earliest writings of the New Testament, the letters of Paul, and one of
the later writings, Luke's Acts of the Apostles, we are introduced to a
number of ordinary women and men doing extraordinary things.

When Paul first enters Europe during his second missionary journey
and passes through the city of Philippi, a local business woman named
Lydia hears him speak and offers her home in a nearby town as a base
for his ministry (Acts 16:11–14). Later on in his journey through
Greece, Paul meets a married couple named Aquila and Priscilla in the
town of Corinth. Initially he stays with them because they are Jews and
because Paul and Aquila are both tentmakers by trade. Later, the pair
accompanies Paul in his travels and eventually head the ministry in the
town of Ephesus in Asia Minor (Acts 18:18–22). The couple's most
notable accomplishment, it seems, was their success in helping another
lay missionary, Apollos, more completely understand "the Way."

Paul usually opens and closes his letters with greetings to and from individuals in the various churches he visited. In these lists of names we once again hear the echo of a time when ministry in the Church was a grassroots movement and not primarily the business of a privileged few. "I commend to you Phoebe our sister, who is (also) a minister of the Church at Cenchreae, that you may receive her in the Lord in a manner worthy of the holy ones, and help her in whatever she may need from you, for she has been a benefactor to many and to me as well. Greet Prisca and Aquila, my co-workers in Christ Jesus, who risked their necks for my life, to whom not only I am grateful but also all the churches of the Gentiles; greet also the church at their house. Greet my beloved Epaenetus, who was the first fruits in Asia for Christ. Greet Mary, who has worked hard for you. Greet Andronicus and Junia, my relatives and my fellow prisoners; they are prominent among the apostles (italics added) and they were in Christ before me" (Romans 16:1–7). Notice that Paul specifically uses the word "apostle" and that ministry seems to be equally shared by women and men. It's also worth noting that he writes "to all God's beloved in Rome" at the beginning of the letter and not to any particular leader.

The Circle of Life

Justin Martyr's description of the celebration of the Eucharist suggests that even one hundred years after Paul this same spirit continued to characterize the local churches. The office of deacon is first mentioned in Acts of the Apostles. (Deaconesses are also known to have existed in the early Church.) Based on the letters to Timothy and Titus—letters attributed to Paul but likely written by a later disciple—it appears that the organizations of local churches varied from place to place almost always including a council of "elders" (*presbyteroi*) along with deacons (*diakonoi*). Sometimes the term bishop (*episkopos*) designated a separate individual responsible for the community—such as Ignatius of Antioch, martyred in 107 AD—and sometimes it seems synonymous with the term *presbyteros* (see Titus 1:5–7). As late as the middle of the third century, there remained an active and equal sharing in the order of the deaconate by both men and women. This is evidenced by the recorded martyrdom of Apollonia, an aged and respected deaconess in the Alexandrian Church.

Even after the offices of bishop, priest, and deacon became "a caste apart" at the end of the third century, the democratic spirit of the early days still thrived. Bishops were not appointed by Rome, or the Emperor, but by popular election in the local church. The most famous example of this practice is the story of St. Ambrose, bishop of Milan from 373 until he died in 397.

About a week before his ordination as bishop, Ambrose was still the pagan Roman governor of the province that included the large city of Milan, Italy. He was a member of the catechumenate—those women and men in the process of study and faith formation on their way to becoming Christians. When the bishop of Milan died earlier in the year, the people turned to Ambrose and by popular acclaim elected him as their new bishop. Ambrose completed his catechetical preparation, received the sacraments of baptism, Holy Communion, and confirmation and was ordained as bishop at a breathtaking pace! While Ambrose's personal circumstances might have been unique, the method of selecting a bishop for even such a large diocese was not unusual.

The Edict of Milan   *313 AD Christian protected by law*

The seeds of a drastic change, however, were planted early in the fourth century. It was a century that started most inauspiciously for the Christian Church. A succession of emperors arising out of the military, and repeated barbarian incursions across the frontiers, had transformed many of the cities of the empire—particularly in the West—into armed fortresses. The Roman economy was in dire straights as a result, and currency devaluations were common. As was true in the time of Decius, this new time of crisis prompted many in the empire to look toward the outrages perpetrated by the Christians against the Roman gods and goddesses as the cause of the empire's troubles.

For a long time, Emperor Diocletian (284–305) stayed his hand. His patience did not stem from a fondness for Christianity, but more from a practical calculation. By the end of the third century, the Christian population was larger than the pagan population in parts of the empire. Even more importantly for the sake of good order, the movement was no longer appealing primarily to the poor and disenfranchised. More and more of the educated and wealthy members of Roman society, those who kept the government functioning, were now

Christians. Finally, in 303, Diocletian gave in to popular sentiments and adopted a similar system to that of Emperor Decian several decades earlier. Once again, any subject or citizen not able to produce the required proof of having made a public sacrifice was subject to imprisonment and execution. When Diocletian retired from public office several years later, however, the persecutions did not end as they had with Decius. The intensity of the persecutions actually increased during the reign of Galerius, one of the four co-rulers who succeeded Diocletian. By 311, the Church had been devasted by the combined effects of the Roman persecutions and the barbarian attacks.

Yet as overwhelming as the attacks against it were, the Church proved to be even more formidable. In 312, the tide finally turned irrevocably in favor of Christianity. At the culmination of a civil war between generals for control of the empire, Constantine prepared to face his rival, Maxentius, near the Milvian Bridge a few miles outside of Rome. During the night before the battle he had a dream.

An ancient author, Lactantius, describes it this way: "Constantine was directed in a dream to mark the Heavenly sign of God on the shields of his soldiers and thus to join battle. He did as he was ordered and with the cross-shaped letter X with its top bent over he marked Christ on the shields" (W.H.C. Frend, p. 123). The next day Constantine won a decisive victory over his rival for the throne. He thus became the sole ruler of the Eastern Roman Empire and, in 324, of the entire empire. In 313, Constantine and the Emperor in the West issued the Edict of Milan which granted Christianity the full protection of Roman law. The era of persecution was over and a new era was beginning.

A Monumental Change

But what would this "new age" be like? It is difficult to put into words the monumental redefinition of how the Church saw itself and its mission in the wake of Constantine's decree. By the time of the fall of the Roman Empire in the West in the fifth century, the Church had been transformed from a counter-cultural, highly diverse, and egalitarian society into the premier secular and spiritual institution of the newly emerging medieval world. We'll consider three significant developments that occurred during this period as a way to gauge the magnitude of the change.

3 Effects of Edict of Milan 313

One tremendous area of development flowed from what might be called the "martyrdom of intention." The days of martyrdom through death and imprisonment had ended, and many zealous souls sought another means to purify all that might be lukewarm in their Christian discipleship. This ever-present need in the human heart for purification—real or exaggerated—was coupled with a growing uneasiness about the meaning of discipleship. Whereas it once it required a great leap of faith and courage to become a Christian, now Christians were living an "ordinary" life, and many were quite wealthy.

It's clear from the teachings of Jesus as presented in the gospels (see Matthew 19:16–30, for example) that Christians had always believed the accumulation of riches would have a deadening effect on the spiritual life. The tradition of packing up and moving out into the desert in order to eliminate all wordly distractions has roots that go back into the ancient Judaism from which Christianity sprouted. The Dead Sea Scrolls, an ancient library of religious texts, very likely belonged to the community of Jewish "monks" who founded the community of Qumran in the middle of the Judean wilderness. It was for this reason that by the end of the second century the wildernesses of Egypt were dotted with hermitages, often caves in which solitary believers spent their lives in prayer and fasting. The most famous of these early hermits was Saint Anthony (251–356) who by the strength of his own personality and zeal attracted many others into this solitary lifestyle. After the Edict of Milan, this monastic movement spread enthusiastically from Egypt into Palestine and then northwest into Asia Minor.

Monastic Communities

It was only natural that this initially solitary form of living would inspire like-minded souls to band together in loosely affiliated hermitages and eventually lead to the formation of more ordered monastic communities. Pachomius (290–345) came up with a basic code of discipline for those gathered around him. Saint Basil (died 379) developed a rule for his monastic community which to this day serves as the basic rule of life for monasteries in the Eastern (Greek Orthodox) Church.

Basil's sister Macrina made her monastery a base for performing the corporal works of mercy—providing food, clothing, shelter, and medical care—to those in the surrounding community. Her example was

① eventual church govt nu
heirarchy like govt

widely copied both in other monastic communities and in the local churches throughout the empire. Often in the declining years of the empire in the West the Church provided the only kind of social "safety net" available to the poor and dispossessed.

For a number of reasons, not the least of which must have been that deserts were rare, the monastic movement developed more slowly in the West. The first great Western monk was Saint Jerome, the patron saint of biblical scholarship because of his efforts in the late fourth century to translate much of the Bible from the Greek language into the common Latin language (Vulgate) of Christians in the West. It's important to note, however, that while Jerome's influence was strongly felt in the West, his hermitage was located just outside of Bethlehem.

East Meets West

Eventually, particularly in the remotest corners of Ireland after the conversion of the Irish to Christianity, monasticism did begin to take hold in the West as well. By the sixth century, monastic orders were a part of the fabric of the Western Church, often the only places of refuge amid the chaos of a crumbling empire.

Saint Benedict of Nursia was concerned that in their zeal to purify themselves of worldly desires, too many monks were doing great harm to their physical, intellectual, emotional, and, consequently spiritual well-being. He developed his own guidelines for monastic life that stressed a balance between prayer, hard work, rest, and recreation. Known as the Rule of Benedict, this became the founding charter for the monastery Benedict founded at Monte Casino around 520—and later for the entire Benedictine order. As was true of Basil's rule in the East, Benedict's rule became the basis for monastic life in the West.

The contributions of the monastic orders to the Church cannot be overstated. Precisely because of their isolation, the monasteries preserved many manuscripts and much learning from antiquity as the growing chaos enveloped Europe. The egalitarian spirit of the early Church survived in the monastery because, just as was true in the local churches of early Christianity, each monastic order took care of its own affairs and elected its own leaders. Monastic orders offered women opportunities to exert control over their own lives and to participate in ministry in ways that were not available to them in general society. And eventually, such as through the reform movement begun at Cluny a few centuries later, monasteries would help guide the Church back from the way of excessive worldliness to the way of the Holy Spirit.

A Time for Reflection *time to think about what they believe*

For individuals and organizations, there is a hierarchy of needs that must be met. Until safety is provided and physical needs are satisfied, it's hard to concentrate on more esoteric pursuits. Just so, once Christians no longer had to fear for their lives, the Church could focus more energy on pondering the mysteries of the faith. This emphasis on reflecting upon and articulating the essential beliefs of the Christian faith was enthusiastically encouraged by Emperor Constantine who wanted the same unanimity of opinion in the Church as he sought in his governance of the empire. And while true consensus was preferred, the emperor was quite willing—in either case—to use the imperial authority to force agreement if necessary.

Myriad beliefs and creative expressions of belief concerning the identity of Jesus, the meaning of his ministry and the role of the Church took shape during these years. Other gospels besides Mark, Matthew, Luke/Acts, and John were circulated. It wasn't until the third century that the New Testament as we know it became known as the "canon" (official list of books) for the Christian Church. It is true, however, that the varieties of "Christianities" that existed in the early centuries of Church history somewhat paralleled the variety of pagan faiths they were replacing. Obviously the limited opportunities for communication (witness Paul's frustration in many of his letters) and the distances between local churches meant that particular beliefs could vary greatly. Even the four canonical gospels present four distinct portraits of Jesus and each has its own unique point of emphasis.

Groundbreaking archeological discoveries of the past century—most notably the Dead Sea Scrolls and the uncovering of a Gnostic Christian library near Nag Hammadi, Egypt—have opened our eyes to just how complex this process of formation of Christian belief was. Followers of Gnosticism, for example, believed that the key to salvation was special knowledge revealed to only a chosen few. Those who converted to Christianity saw in Jesus' teachings the wisdom that they sought. Given their belief that all matter including the human body was inherently corrupt, however, they could not accept the idea that Jesus was ever really a human being. This mixture of Gnostic and more orthodox ("right thinking") Christian beliefs led to the heresy of Docetism. Docetists believed that Jesus' humanity was only an illusion, similar to the stories in Greek and Roman mythology of gods and god- *heresy* desses who temporarily assumed human form.

From the other direction came expressions of Christianity that called into question Jesus' divinity. Arianists (named after bishop Arius of Alexandria, whose struggles with the orthodox bishop Athanasius are the stuff of legends) believed that Jesus was fully human but some sort of a demi-god subordinate to God the Father. At one point in the fourth century, it is likely there were more Arian Christians than those who believed in the full humanity and divinity of Jesus. Variations on Arianist tendencies included Modalism, the belief that God became the three persons of the Trinity successively but not simultaneously, and Monophysitism, which held that the divine nature of Jesus absorbed his human nature. (This heresy is the basis for the split between the Egyptian Coptic Church from mainstream Christianity.) There were also major schisms within Christendom that had less to do with doctrine and more to do with practice. As you might recall, the Church of the Martyrs, more commonly known as the Donatists, had roots that went back to the time of the Decian persecution and the belief that sacraments ministered by lapsed bishops, priests, or deacons were not valid.

The Council of Nicea *one in being with the Father AD 325*

Having restored political unity to the empire in the first part of the fourth century, Emperor Constantine sought to bring unity to the varying interpretations of the Christian faith. He (not the bishops) called for a council to be held in Nicea, a town not far away from the new capital city of Constantinople. The result of that council was the brief summation of Christian beliefs known as the Nicene Creed. It survives as the profession of faith made by Catholics every Sunday. In an attempt to respond to the growing Arian controversy, the creed invoked a non-scriptural word when it proclaimed that the Son (Jesus) was "one in being" (*homousios*) with the Father. (The fallout caused by this one little word is part of the story in Chapter Four.)

The work of Nicea did not put an end to the controversy and confusion. The orthodox position that Jesus was both fully human and fully divine was further clarified a century later when, at the Council of

Ephesus in 431, Mary was identified as *theotokos*, the bearer of God. Finally, the Council of Chalcedon in 451 came up with the definitive expression of the Christian understanding of the Incarnation, the basis of all other Christian beliefs: "We confess that one and the same Lord Jesus Christ, the only-begotten Son, must be acknowledged in two natures, without confusion or change, without division or separation. The distinction between the natures was never abolished by their union, but rather the character proper to each of the two natures was preserved as they came together in one person and one *hypostasis.* (See John 1:1–18 or Philippians 2:5–11 for a more beautiful expression of the Mystery.)

The Fall and Rise of the Roman Empire

There's an episode of *Star Trek* in which Captain Kirk and his crewmates visit a planet in which the Roman Empire never fell. In fact, that's exactly what did happen, but not in the way the creators of Star Trek envisioned. The third major effect of the Edict of Milan was the transformation in the way the "body of Christ" saw its mission and identity. As the bishops took on more and more secular power and influence, the gap between clergy and laity widened to enormous proportions.

The fourth century was the time when the rising power and influence of the Church and the declining power and influence of the empire, especially in the West, intersected. From the time of the Edict of Milan, which made Christianity a *legal* religion in the empire, to the time of Emperor Theodosius I who declared Christianity to be the *only* religion of the empire, the Church and state worked mostly harmoniously. (The years of Emperor Julian's reign from 361 to 363 is a notable exception to this.)

These were the decades in which the first large churches were built modeled on the style of the basilica, the large, three part buildings in which the emperors and governors presided. Bishops in the largest dioceses, a Roman administrative territory roughly equivalent to a county, began to command a great deal of power and influence in civil matters as well as religious ones. (A good example of this shift is Bishop Ambrose's letter to Emperor Theodosius, which was highly critical of a massacre the emperor carried out in the city of Thessalonica.) Many of the vestments we commonly associate with bishops, priests, and deacons today originated as the dress of Roman aristocrats.

By the advent of the fifth century, however, the balance of power in the West had clearly shifted. The waves of barbarian invasions that had battered the empire intermittently in the third and fourth centuries now became a steady barrage; more and more emperors concentrated on preserving what was left in the East from their capital city of Constantinople and left the Western provinces to their individual fates. In 410, the unthinkable happened when Rome was sacked by barbarian invaders under the leadership of Alaric. The Western capital shifted from Rome to the city of Ravenna, a place easier to defend because of its geographic location. A generation before the last emperor in the West was deposed by the barbarian invaders in 476, virtually all imperial power and rule in the West had disintegrated.

At the same time that the Western Empire was crumbling, the decentralized, lay movement that was the early Church had been completely transformed into something that looked, institutionally at least, very much like the Roman imperial government it was now replacing. In the midst of all of the chaos, the Church was the only institution with the resources necessary to cope with the tremendous needs of millions of people suffering from the famine, dispossession, and grinding poverty that accompanied the collapse of civil order. Bishops took on more and more of the functions of the non-existent Roman governors.

This was especially true in the case of the bishop of Rome. Pope Damasus (366–84) is the first pope known to have explicitly claimed the primacy of the bishop of Rome over all other bishops, just as the emperor reigned supreme over his governors. During this time it became customary to refer to the pope with a title formerly reserved for the emperor: "Pontifex Maximus," literally the "Great Bridge" between God and human beings. This title survives today in the word "Pontiff."

In many less obvious ways, Roman methods of governing had deeply penetrated the hierarchy of the Church by the end of the fifth century. Canon (Church) law was codified based on the laws of the empire. More democratic means of choosing bishops were replaced by either papal appointments or appointments by civil rulers. The line between Church and state had almost completely dissolved.

Augustine and Leo

Although the morphing of the Church from an essentially counter-cultural movement into the civil and spiritual authority of the ancient world would have grave consequences in centuries to come, the major impetus was actually very pastoral. Just as Jesus reached out time and time again to the poor and marginalized, so did the Church in an effort to provide some level of comfort and security to the faithful. When Attila the Hun led his minions to the gates of Rome in 441, for example, the only one there to meet him was Pope Leo I. Using skills of diplomacy and persuasion, Leo was able to convince Attila not to sack the city. During his long pontificate that lasted until 461, Leo used the extensive resources of the Church to care for the immense numbers of needy in Rome, as well as to steadily extend the power and influence of the papacy throughout the Christian world. The decree on the Incarnation from the Council of Chalcedon was greatly influenced by a letter written by this pope, known as the "Tome of Leo."

While Pope Leo I was exerting his influence in more practical matters, another bishop, Augustine of Hippo (354–430), was laying much of the theological groundwork in the West. The story of Augustine's dramatic conversion is told in his autobiography, *The Confessions*, which is widely considered one of the great works of Christian literature. Augustine was involved in all of the major crises concerning Church doctrine during the fifth century, including dealings with the schismatic Church of the Martyrs in North Africa. His explorations of the Christian belief in the Trinity (*De Trinitatae*) is a profound meditation on how the Trinity is the fullest expression of God's boundless love for creation in general and humanity in particular.

The other great work of Augustine, *De Civitate Dei* (*City of God*), was written in part to provide comfort to Christians living through the disintegration of the Roman Empire. He reassures the faithful that this turn of events did not mean the pagans were right in accusing the Church of offending the gods, but rather that all human kingdoms, however grand, are merely transitory. The city of God, on the other hand, is composed of those true believers who are united with Christ and his Church through their faith and who are brought to perfection by God's grace. The city of God would not be fully revealed in all its glory until the end of time, however. In the meantime, Augustine warned in another of his works, as you may recall: "There are some that God has that the Church does not have, and there are some that the Church has that God does not have."

Unfortunately, we will see that as the power and influence of the Church grew during the Middle Ages, this was a piece of advice often ignored. The powerful, wealthy, and increasingly hierarchical Church that emerged from the collapse of the Western Empire and that provided the basic social, spiritual, and often political superstructure of Medieval Europe had little in common with those small diffuse communities of Christians who characterized the body of Christ during the three centuries following the death and resurrection of Jesus of Nazareth. And while the same Holy Spirit that blew through the Church on the first Pentecost continued to blow up a storm, too often the spiritual authority of the Church would be compromised by a grasping for money and power at the expense of genuine openness to change.

For Thought and Discussion

1) Read again the description of the celebration of the Eucharist written by Justin the Martyr. How many of the particular parts can you identify in the celebration of the Eucharist today?

2) What point do you think Jesus was making in the cleansing of the temple? In what ways do you think the "temple" of institutional religion need to be cleansed today?

3) Discuss some of the advantages and disadvantages of selecting Church leaders the way Ambrose was selected. Would you recommend the revival of this practice? Why or why not?

4) Why do you think monasticism grew so explosively after the Edict of Milan? In what ways can lay people today incorporate the monastic practice of withdrawal from the world?

5) What is your understanding of who Jesus is and what the Church is. What are the turning points in your own life that have deepened your insight into both?

6) How would you describe the contributions of Pope Leo the Great and Augustine to the Church. (Use one or two of the sources cited in the bibliography to get more information.)

7) How do you understand the term *sensus fidelium* in the time period discussed in this chapter? What was the relationship between leadership and the laity?

Part Two

The Medieval Church

 FOUR

The Eastern Schism

Deep-seated changes on the earth's surface can happen quickly or slowly. When a volcano explodes or the earth's crust is torn by an earthquake, the landscape can be altered overnight. Yet the forces of erosion take millennia to shape the contours of the earth. The two greatest divisions, or schisms, to rip the fabric of Christendom through the centuries reflect these distinct processes in an analogous way. The second, the Protestant Reformation, produced massive changes within a generation. The first one happened much more gradually as relations between the Eastern and the Western halves of the Church eroded over time. Somewhere along the way, the two faith communities stopped speaking the same language, literally at first and then spiritually as well. The anatomy of this split, known as the Great Eastern Schism, and its profound effect on the development of the Church is the subject of this chapter.

Two Different Languages

Because of the nature of the split, it's difficult to isolate one great turning point. Even by the time of the Council of Nicea in the fourth century, it was becoming clear that the Greek language of the Eastern Roman Empire and the Latin of the West were making it difficult for bishops and theologians to communicate with one another. When it came to the complicated matters of formulating Church doctrine, much was being lost in the translation. This was most obvious in the controversy that ensued after the Greek word *homousios* was included in the final formulation of the Nicene Creed. This word described the Son of God and second person of the Trinity as "one in being with" the Father.

For the first time, a fundamental formulation of Christian belief included a word not found in the Scriptures. Naturally such a decision affecting the core Christian belief in the Trinity came under extreme scrutiny and deliberation before, during, and after the conclusion of the Council of Nicea in 325. Attempts among bishops from both East and West to work through particular theological difficulties and ambiguities were hampered because of inadequate translations from Greek to Latin and Latin to Greek.

The exact meaning of the Greek and Latin words for "person" and "substance," for example, could not be clearly translated. As a result, Latin prayers and definitions based on the Creed, which affirmed that we encounter the one true God as three distinct *persons*, was sometimes misunderstood in the East as suggesting that God's being included three distinct *substances*. What might seem like a matter of semantics to us suggested to many in the Eastern Church that bishops in the West had succumbed to the heresy of monophysitism, a rejection of the Christian belief that Jesus was a unique person with both a human and a divine nature. This was a heresy that bedeviled the Easterners for centuries.

The Rise of Islam

A dramatic blow to East-West unity came as a by-product of the greatest spiritual movement of the seventh and eighth centuries. It all started in 610 when a Middle Eastern caravan trader of no particular importance found himself caught up in a powerful experience of what he (and millions of Muslims since) believe to have been divine inspiration. The words that Muhammad ibn Abdulla brought back from his encounter with the divine—words that would be recorded in precise Arabic detail in the Qur'an—touched off a spiritual, cultural, and political revolution that began in the trading towns of the Arabian Peninsula. By 630, it was beginning to spread rapidly throughout the entire Middle East. The fledgling religious faith of Islam spread with an intensity and ferociousness that caught the Christian world completely by surprise.

In 635, the Byzantine Empire responded to the overwhelmingly successful Muslim conquests in a pitched battle fought at least as much for political reasons as for religious ones. The Byzantine effort to retain control of the cradle of the Christian faith in Palestine and Syria failed quite dramatically, however, when its army was soundly defeated by a Muslim force half its size near the Yarmuk river in modern-day Jordan. In 637, Jerusalem fell, ensuring the total domination of the Muslims in the Holy Land.

The rest of the seventh century saw formerly Christian lands fall to the Muslim forces. Egypt received the Muslims without much resistance, in part because the teachings of the Qur'an about the one true God seemed very much like the teachings of the Monophysite heresy that had so many adherents there. The North African Church, once the most dynamic and vital faith community in the West, had never really recovered from the Donatist schism (see Chapter Two) and the attacks of the Vandals several centuries earlier. By the time the Muslim expansion was checked in Europe, North Africa was once again a stronghold of religious faith. Now, however, the faith was Islam. Constantinople and the entire region of Asia Minor barely fended off a Muslim invasion in 669.

A Century of Conquest

As the seventh century drew to a close, Islamic forces had crossed the straights of Gibraltar into Spain. The grand effect of this century of conquest was to virtually cut off all communication between the Western and now largely reduced Eastern portions of the Christian Church. By the time Frankish forces led by Charles Martel finally stopped the advances of the Muslim forces at the battle of Tours in 732, the Western Church had become a kind of lifeboat adrift in a sea of Islamic kingdoms to the South, the remnants of the Byzantine Empire to the East, and barbarian tribes to the north. Any lingering illusions of eastern hegemony in the West evaporated as both parts of the Church struggled simply to survive.

Responding to Christ's commission to make disciples of all the nations now meant that this increasingly Roman Catholic Church would have to continue the mission of conversion and evangelization among the barbarian tribes which bordered the lands of the now defunct Western Roman Empire. The mission to Britian and Ireland had its roots in the efforts of such notables as Patrick and Brigid of Kildare two centuries before. The enterprise received a new impetus and new organization, however, during the time of Pope Gregory the Great (590–604). Gregory sent Augustine to Canterbury, and through his efforts that city became the seat of the Christian Church in Britain and a base camp from which missionary activities could be coordinated. The Synod of Whitby in 664 greatly increased the establishment of Roman Catholicism in Britian. (We'll take a more detailed look at Gregory's pontificate in the next chapter.)

In the eighth century the focus of the Church's missionary activities was the heartland of the Germanic tribes. These were the peoples who in Roman times had fiercely resisted the incursions of the Roman legions and for the most part maintained their independence. Unlike the Britons and the Celts, the Germanic tribes did not have an extensive previous experience with Christianity that the missionaries could build on. Still, the conversion of the Franks in the fifth century was at least a beginning. The two most notable of the missionaries to the Germans are Boniface and his female cousin Lioba, who together courageously helped the Christian faith to take root. The series of convents and monasteries established laid the groundwork for an organized, peaceful evangelization and conversion of the Germanic peoples. This mix of cultures within the Western Church would come to be yet another point of distinction between the Roman Catholic Church and the more homogeneous Church of the East.

While these major sea changes within the East and West were occurring, a more basic cause of division had already played itself out. After the Western Roman Empire collapsed in 476, the lands formerly ruled by the emperor deteriorated into a patchwork of petty barbarian kingdoms by the sixth and seventh centuries. In theory the West remained under the control of Constantinople through the emperor's representatives in Ravenna, Italy. In fact, however, those officials lacked the means to enforce their authority. For a short time, Emperor Justinian the Great (483–565) succeeded in reasserting Roman rule in Sicily and the southern Italian peninsula, but that resurgence of imperial power was cut short by the growing threat of the Lombards moving in from the north toward Rome.

Forging Deals

Faced with the unpleasant political realities confronting him, the bishop of Rome and the rest of the Church hierarchy in the West needed to make deals among the warring barbarian nations surrounding them in order to safeguard Christian lives and Church property. The most significant such alliance during this period, often referred to as the Dark Ages, was that forged in 753 between Pope Stephen II and the son of Charles Martel, king of the Franks. In an act of diplomatic ingenuity that would have made Leo the Great proud, Stephen made the arduous crossing of the Alps in order to make his appeal to Pepin the Short in person. Pepin was so honored that after he successfully defended Rome against the Lombards and defeated them, he granted the bishop of Rome a wide strip of land spanning the center of the Italian peninsula. These estates would serve as a buffer zone between Rome and any hostile powers in the vicinity for the next thousand years. Eventually this donation of Pepin would come to be known as the Papal States.

Stephen's decision to cozy up to the Franks made a lot of sense from a Western point of view. Ever since their mass conversion during the time of the Merovingian dynasty in the waning days of the Western Roman Empire, the Franks stood out as an early success story of Christian missionary activity among the barbarians. (Keep in mind, however, that a "mass conversion" had little to do with the kind of personal "metanoia" Jesus calls for in the gospels and a lot to do with the will of the particular absolute monarch who happened to be in power at the time.) Turning to the Franks in time of dire need seemed a natural progression in the relationship between the Franks and the Church.

The emperor in the East, however, saw things quite differently. Upon hearing about Pepin's "donation," the Byzantine ruler reacted angrily. As far as he was concerned, the *entire* Italian peninsula, and all of Gaul for that matter, belonged to the empire. What right did Pepin have to grant those lands to anyone? Even worse, what right did the bishop of Rome have to accept this donation? Certainly he should have known better.

In 800, when Pope Leo III added insult to injury by crowning Pepin's son, Charlemagne, as the first Holy Roman Emperor, Byzantine annoyance at the pope's impertinence hardened into fury at the pope's blatant act of treason.

pope – emperor – who is in charge

The Iconoclasm Crisis

From the time of Emperor Constantine, the concerns of the civil rulers in the East and the concerns of the bishop of Constantinople—known as the Patriarch—were so intertwined that inevitably a rift between pope and emperor would become a rift between pope and patriarch. In the ninth century the emphasis shifted from the political to the theological over two issues. The first was the Iconoclasm crisis. This 150-year intermittent struggle primarily between the Byzantine Emperor and the monasteries of the Eastern Church is mostly a footnote in the history of the West. Yet there would not be any serious and sustained movement toward healing the schism between East and West for over a thousand years after this particular storm had passed.

From the times of the early Church, the use of images in painting, mosaic, and sculpture to express and inspire belief among Christians is well established. These images—in Greek, *icons*—included representations of Christ, Mary, the apostles and early martyrs, angels, and also illustrations of events in the Bible. While there have been abuses at times in the way such images were promoted and understood, Christian spirituality has generally embraced these works of art. If God would take on human flesh as the belief in the Incarnation maintained, then it naturally followed that all creation has been infused with a particular sacredness. Artistic representations help the believer see this sacredness more clearly and help focus his or her heart and mind on the mysteries of faith.

Suddenly, in the eighth century, this traditional position of the Church toward icons changed drastically in the East. The exact reasons for Emperor Leo III's call in 725 for the destruction of icons throughout the empire is unclear. Perhaps it was the influence of his Muslim neighbors who now bordered the lands of his truncated empire. (It is strictly forbidden in the Islamic faith to create any images of God.) There were a few bishops in the East who supported the emperor in his decision, but not many.

Theology Wars

By 730, the movement had gained such momentum that the Patriarch of Constantinople, an opponent of this icon smashing or "iconoclasm," was forced to resign. He was replaced by Anastasius (730–41), a man more amenable to the emperor's way of thinking. For a long time the edicts prohibiting icons and ordering either their destruction or their covering up were applied sporadically until Leo's successor, Constantine V, laid out a supposed theological basis for iconoclasm that raised it from simply a policy of the emperor to a duty of conscience for every believer. It went something like this: representations of Christ separated his two indivisible natures by attempting to portray one in isolation from the other. Icons in general could also be seen as attempts to define and limit the supernatural and incomprehensible aspects of divine mysteries. No doubt through a good degree of arm-twisting and well placed political appointments, the emperor succeeded in having this understanding confirmed by a council of bishops. All who disagreed—including the previous Patriarch, Germanicus, and the great John Damascene—were declared to be heretics.

Up to this point, the Western Church seems to have paid little attention to the controversy. When the writings of John Damascene defending the veneration of icons reached Rome, however, Pope Gregory II (731–41) sent a formal letter of protest to both the emperor and the patriarch. A Roman synod of bishops added its own voice of protest. This open break in communion with the emperor, who as the successor of Constantine the Great still saw himself as the protector and benefactor of the entire Church, was viewed with great hostility by the civil and religious ruling elite in the East. Most significantly, it was the first time that the patriarch and pope had declared open opposition to the other's position. Even after the crisis reached its apogee and gradually fizzled out in the first half of the ninth century, memories of this confrontation endured. One more straw and the camel's back would break.

The Schism Begins

That straw was the Latin word *filioque*, the Latin phrase added to the Nicene Creed in the West, which stated that the Holy Spirit proceeded from the Father *and from the Son*. At least as far back as 589, when a council of Spanish bishops at Toledo accepted the change, the phrase had become a part of the lexicon in the West. In fact, most Western bishops and theologians believed it had been implicit in the Nicene Creed all along. Remember, however, that it was primarily in the East where the intense debate that culminated in the Nicene Creed took place. The idea that the work of a mere local council in one region of the Church could alter such an essential expression of Christian belief, without the approval of the entire (ecumenical) assembly of bishops, was a terrible affront to Eastern sensibilities.

This implicit rejection of the Western position became explicit in the 860s after Photius was installed by Emperor Michael III as patriarch of Constantinople. When Pope Nicholas I denounced Photius's succession as illegitimate—the emperor had deposed the previous patriarch simply because the bishop had displeased him—the new patriarch was inspired by the slight to denounce what in his way of seeing things was the plethora of heresies being practiced and approved of by the bishop of Rome. Most particularly, Photius took issue with the addition of the phrase *filioque* to the creed. The immediate crisis these cross-denunciations caused was eliminated when a few years later the emperor deposed Photius, but it would turn out that relations between pope and patriarch had been irrevocably shattered.

In 1043, Patriarch Michael Cerularius went beyond the traditional understanding in the East that the patriarch of Constantinople and the Bishop of Rome were equals. Given the pope's position on the *filioque* crisis and his support of the illegitimate rulers of the so-called Holy Roman Empire (remember from an Eastern point of view there already was an emperor), Patriarch Michael believed the Bishop of Rome could no longer be relied upon to preserve and protect the Christian faith. In a move without precedent in the East or West, the patriarch claimed that he was in fact the spiritual successor of Peter, and he began to make policy decisions intended not just for Constantinople but for Rome as well. Pope Leo IX sent Cardinal Humbert to Constantinople in the hopes of working out some sort of an understanding with his fellow bishop.

Ninety Heresies

Leo's intentions were good but his choice of ambassador was awful. Cardinal Humbert came to Constantinople not with a list of talking points, but with a list of more than ninety heresies for which he held the patriarch personally responsible! Needless to say, the enormous arrogance of both men made any meaningful discussion impossible. Before Humbert left in a huff on July 16, 1054, he stopped off at the most ancient and venerated church in the city, Hagia Sophia, and deposited a bull of excommunication on the church's main altar. The patriarch responded by excommunicating Cardinal Humbert as well.

It's hard to imagine how this story could get more bizarre, but it does. When Cardinal Humbert returned to Rome, he learned that pope Leo IX had died three months earlier. Any appointments the pope makes automatically cease to exist at the moment of his death. This meant that Cardinal Humbert lacked the authority to excommunicate anyone from anything. The drama of the conflict eclipsed the actual facts of the situation in popular imagination, however, so the designation of July 16, 1054, as the "official" beginning of the Eastern Schism endures. *1054*

The final, most tragic blow to relations between the now separated Roman Catholic and Eastern, or Greek, Orthodox Churches happened in the thirteenth century. This was the end of the era of the Crusades, "Holy Wars" initiated by a series of popes and aimed at reclaiming the ancient Christian lands from Muslim control. (We will explore the idea of holy war in Chapter Seven.) The discipline and focus of the Crusaders diminished with each campaign. By the time of the fourth Crusade, any genuine spiritual motivation had mostly been replaced by greed for wealth and treasure. No city enjoyed a greater reputation for wealth and treasure than Constantinople, which had remained the capital of the Eastern Roman, or Byzantine, Empire for almost a thousand years.

When Pope Innocent III caught wind of the Crusaders' true intentions, he forbade them from attacking Constantinople under penalty of excommunication. The pope's prohibitions went unheeded, however, when in 1204, the troops committed a sacking and looting of the Byzantine capital that exceeded anything the barbarian tribes had done in ancient times. Although the pope had not given the attack his blessing, the centuries of ill will and the close association of the Church with the Crusades convinced the laity and clergy of the East otherwise. The desire of Jesus "that all may be one," always a challenge for the Church to incarnate in itself, would remain unheeded in East-West relations for almost one thousand years.

Collective Amnesia

When asked to describe the greatest split in the history of the Church, most Roman Catholics would probably point to the Protestant Reformation. And yet the fundamental deformity in the body of Christ that occurred as a result of the split between East and West makes all of the issues and conflicts connected with the Protestant Reformation pale in comparison. Consider for a few moments the scope of this enormous schism.

Imagine a circle in your mind. This is a picture of the Christian Church in the fourth century. Just as the Mediterranean Sea was called a Roman lake, so it could also be called a Christian one, as all the lands of Europe, Asia, and Africa surrounding it were overwhelmingly Christian.

Now, fold the circle in half. Most of the lands in the lower half of the circle were lost to Christianity in the Muslim conquests of the seventh century. Divide what's left in half again and take away one part, symbolizing the Eastern Schism. From this point on in our study of the turning points in Church history, we'll need to put an asterisk next to the word "Church." The story of Roman Catholicism, in essence, is the story of about twenty-five percent of the Christian world as it manifested itself in the early Church. For almost the next thousand years after the schism, the history of the Church and of Western Europe would be virtually synonymous. Only within the last one hundred years or so can we make any meaningful claim of being once again "catholic."

The implication of all of this is staggering. Look again at the names of the early Church fathers and mothers who helped shape the body of Christ in the first four or five centuries of Church history. How many of the great spiritual leaders and thinkers of that period are from the cradle of Christianity in the East? Some names that come to mind include: Basil and his sister Macrina, their brother Gregory of Nyssa (talk about good genes!), Gregory of Naziansus, deaconess Appollonia of Alexandria, and bishops Polycarp of Smyrna and Ignatius of Antioch. Of course, virtually every woman and man in the original apostolic generation were from the East, including Mary Magdalene and Peter himself.

Consider further that all of the Church councils including Nicaea and Chalcedon, which grappled with the formulations of fundamental Christian beliefs, although ecumenical (world-wide), were predominantly composed of eastern bishops and theologians. When the Western Church became a lifeboat we lost touch to a significant degree with our own catholic history. This schism has afflicted us in the West with a form of amnesia that sometimes prevents us from seeing ourselves as a product of historical, cultural, and spiritual development infused with the presence of the Holy Spirit. This collective amnesia makes us prey to the ecclesial fundamentalism defined in the beginning of this book. It was a major concern of Vatican Council II (see Chapter Eight).

The Nature of Faith

The Eastern Schism has also affected our understanding of faith in the West. Rooted in the earliest experience of the Resurrection, Eastern spirituality tended to understand faith as an ongoing relationship with God. As with the first witnesses to the risen Christ, our experience of Christ individually and as a faith community always precedes our ability to formulate particular doctrines and dogmas. The Nicene Creed could only come into being after centuries of *experiencing* Christian discipleship; Christian discipleship never comes through the imposition of any creed. Those first disciples of Jesus who would come to be known as Christians found themselves drawn together by a radically new experience of God. The stories of the Resurrection and the Pentecost event attempt to translate this historical and spiritual experience into words.

Although there developed a rich mystical tradition in the West, thanks to the efforts of such passionate people as Teresa of Avila and John of the Cross, the Western understanding of faith has tended to be more practical. Time and time again we speak of the "deposit of faith"— the implication being that faith can more properly be viewed as an "it" rather than as a process or relationship. "Handing on the faith" has more to do, therefore, with making sure that specific doctrines and dogmas are clear and that the particular means of communicating those belief statements through liturgy and catechesis from one generation to the next always emphasize accuracy over creativity. (Hence the stubborn survival of the *Baltimore Catechism* method of religious education.)

Clearly, history has played a role here. For centuries, popes in the West had their hands full fending off one barbarian tribe or another, an environment that did not allow for much quiet reflection on the great mystery at the center of our Church. But the East has also suffered from the schism. The full effects of this split on the Eastern Church are outside the scope of this book, but it is worth noting now that the hard-won independence from temporal rulers and their ambitions achieved to a great degree in the West never happened in an Eastern Church dominated by the emperors for so many years. The point is not, however, to figure out which church got it right and which one didn't. It's much closer to the truth to say, with apologies to Mahatma Gandhi, that East and West are like the two eyes of the Church. To see Jesus in three-dimensions requires us to see him through both eyes together.

The Light on the Horizon

At the time, it was mostly a footnote to Vatican Council II. As he was bringing the fourth and final session of the council to a close on December 7, 1965, Pope Paul VI lifted the excommunication levied against Patriarch Michael by Cardinal Humbert in 1054. This symbolic act, coupled with a similar action taken by the Patriarch of Constantinople, sent a clear message to the people of the Eastern Catholic (Orthodox) and Roman Catholic Churches: We are brothers and sisters in Christ. It is a message that was amplified and expanded upon during the papacy of Pope John Paul II, as exemplified by the pope's words in his encyclical at the close of Jubilee Year 2000, *Novo Millennio Ineunte* (Sect. 48): "May the memory of the time when the Church breathed with 'both lungs' spur Christians of East and West to walk together in unity of faith and with respect for legitimate diversity, accepting and sustaining each other as members of the one Body of Christ."

Clearly the effects of all these centuries of separation will take time to overcome. Yet in the actions of the magisterium, supported overwhelmingly by the Catholic laity, we see the beginnings of a new *sensus fidei* toward the other members of our fractured Christian family. What this movement toward ecumenism—toward the East and also toward more recently separated brothers and sisters—will look like in the future and what forms it will take are known only to the Holy Spirit. It's certain, however, that as the Church changes its mind, we will open ourselves up to spiritual graces and horizons beyond our imagination. Perhaps at times God tolerates these terrible breaches in communion so that Christians might again and again discover how much they need one another.

For Thought and Discussion

1) Review the significance of each of the following in the development of the Eastern Schism:
   • theological debates over *homousios* and *filioque*
   • the fall of the Western Roman Empire
   • the rise of Islam
   • iconoclasm
   • the events of 1054
   • the sacking of Constantinople

2) "Faith that cannot be clearly defined is Faith that has not been really experienced." What is your reaction to this statement, and why?

3) There are a number of mostly small Eastern Churches that are culturally distinct but in full communion with the Roman Catholic Church (for example, Byzantine and Chaldean Churches). Do some research on the history, beliefs, and liturgical practices of one or more of these churches.

4) Have you personally been aware of the effects of the Eastern Schism on the development of the Roman Catholic Church? In what ways?

5) Was the split between the Eastern and Western Churches unavoidable? Give specific reasons to support your opinion. What conclusions can you draw from your analysis?

6) Vatican Council II called for a renewed effort toward ecumenism (reuniting Christians) and interfaith dialogue. How important a priority do you think this is for the Church today? Why?

7) Discuss the interaction of the magisterium and the faithful in forming the *sensus fidei* during this period.

FIVE

"Rebuild My Church"

It's a well-known story. The young Francis of Assisi, a wealthy aristo-crat having returned home from battle because of illness, visits the ruins of the church dedicated to Saint Damiano and hears a message from God: "Rebuild my Church." In his innocence and simplicity, Francis begins the task of restoring the building. God's calling, of course, was much more ambitious.

The last century before the turn of the first millennium was not the best of times for the Church. This was true for a wide variety of reasons, especially the collapse of any remnants of imperial order as the Holy Roman Empire fell into ruins soon after the death of Charlemagne. Effective leadership within the Church virtually ceased to exist.

Here's a sense of things:

> Pope Boniface VII (984–85) had his predecessor, Benedict VI, strangled, stole the papal bank account and fled to Constantinople, hoping to buy the services of the Byzantines in his struggle against Emperor Otto II. When Otto II died, Boniface returned and imprisoned the newly elected Pope John XIV, who died of poisoning while in prison. (Anthony E. Gilles, *The People of Faith*)

Change some of the names in this quote and you have an episode of a modern crime drama!

The chaos of the time, commonly referred to as the Dark Ages in the West, left many local churches with corrupt or ineffectual leadership and the papacy in chaos. For a time after the collapse of the empire in the West, the little order and few social "safety nets" that did exist were due in large part to the influence of good Church leaders. As Jesus did with the loaves and fish, these men tapped into the spiritual power behind the material and made limited resources go a long way for the common good. The contributions of Pope Leo I were briefly sketched in Chapter Three.

About a century later, Pope Gregory I (590–604), who preferred the title "servant of the servants of God," led the Herculean efforts required to establish hospitals and orphanages and arrange for the care and housing of the poor. At the same time, he was strengthening the independence of the Church in the West from the political ambitions of the Eastern, or Byzantine, emperors. Gregory reformed the liturgy, instituting the type of antiphonal chanting that still bears his name. He acted on Jesus' command to "make disciples of all nations" by inaugurating a vigorous missionary ministry into the lands of the Germanic tribes and even farther northward on the European continent.

Times Were Changing

While the crowning of Charlemagne as the first Holy Roman Emperor in 800 AD gave hope that the stability of the Western Roman Empire could be restored in a more truly Christianized version, the reforms Charlemagne actually initiated could not be sustained much beyond his death. Inevitably, the papacy succumbed to the chaos enveloping much of Western Europe, the heartland of the Roman Catholic Church.

Things were changing in other fundamental ways as well. The most significant change affected the system of feudalism, in which landed estates were controlled by a few nobles whose vassals were responsible for the millions of serfs bound to the lands of their birth for the rest of their lives.

In the five centuries following the collapse of the Western Empire, feudalism had become the dominant social and economic structure of Western Europe—and of the dioceses of the Roman Catholic Church. In the two centuries following the turn of the first millennium, however, the various farmer's markets and county seats dotting the countryside began to grow into the first large towns and cities seen in Western Europe since the fall of Rome. This growth was partially fueled by and gave impetus to the development of a large merchant class and the development of guilds to protect and organize the interests and needs of various craftsmen. While life on a feudal manor for the serfs was difficult and generally short, at least they could usually count on eking out a subsistence existence on the small plots of land allotted to each family. As the size of towns and cities grew, so did the usual problems associated with an urban population: homelessness, hunger, poverty and alienation.

Finally, in part as an unintended consequence of the Crusades, Western Europeans were beginning to be reintroduced to their intellectual heritage as the great writings in mathematics, science, literature, and philosophy of the Greeks and Romans were brought back via the Muslim cultures that had preserved them in Arabic. The educational reforms Charlemagne had envisioned began to take shape, and they inspired a rethinking of the meaning of life and of humanity's place in the universe—and thus what it meant to be the body of Christ. This time, fundamental changes in the Church would mostly come from the bottom up, with the laity and clergy working among the people leading the way.

The Mendicants *Franciscans* *to beg*

Responding to Jesus' admonition, "Just as you did it to one of the least of these who are members of my family, you did it to me" (Matthew 25:40), the Church had made great efforts to meet the needs of the poor and the sick in the dioceses of the empire and later in the various fiefdoms that arose in the wake of the empire's collapse. Ways and means of addressing these needs varied greatly. Sometimes the local bishops were directly involved, as reflected in the legend of Saint Nicholas, bishop of Smyrna in the fourth century. It is said that he would leave anonymous gifts for the poor in order to avoid embarrassing them. (This is the origin of the Santa Claus story.) Other efforts were more formal, such as the establishment of the first hospitals by Pope Gregory I. Often monasteries and convents would serve as places of refuge for the local populace in times of war, and they would offer whatever rudimentary medical care might be available.

What all of these methods had in common, however, was a certain level of "loving detachment." Those who ministered to the poor genuinely cared about them, but for the most part lived privileged lives in comparison with the rest of the local population. They could help the poor but could never really understand what it was like to *be* poor. The times demanded the need for what we today would call an "urban apostolate" of men and women who, as Jesus did, would live with the poor, eat with them, and thus gain an insider's view of their hopes, dreams, and most pressing needs.

This call of the Spirit was articulated in the twelfth century in particular by three people: Francis Bernadone (1182–1226), his close friend Clare di Favarone (1193–1252), and Dominic de Guzman (1170–1221). They are the founders of three of the mendicant religious orders that survive to this day: Franciscans, Poor Clares, and Dominicans. Francis's conversion from a life of wealth and nobility to a very public (and very naked!) denunciation of both is well documented and is probably second only to that of the conversion of Paul as far as stories of dramatic transformations go.

Soon after his conversion, he set out to preach the gospel to the poor, living only on what the generosity of the people of Assisi and the surrounding area would supply him. (The Latin root of the word "mendicant" means "to beg.") Francis's efforts to articulate this urban apostolate were so radical that many of the citizens of Assisi, including his own family, could not understand them. For a time there was a real danger that Francis would be arrested and locked away for his efforts— and successes—in enticing other young people to embrace what seemed to be his particular brand of insanity.

Despite the popularity of Francis's ministry among the poor of Assisi over the next decade, the Church hierarchy was slow to recognize his request for a formal charter of a religious order that would come to be known as the Franciscans. Partly this was because the magisterium is naturally prudent in allowing time for the full effects of new movements or forms of spirituality to be seen. "By their fruits you shall know them," as Jesus said. But this hesitancy also reflects a kind of "bottom up" movement of the Holy Spirit. It would not be until 1223, a few years before Francis died, that the religious order he founded would be formally recognized by Pope Innocent III. Despite explosive growth and many changes in the order's original charter—not all of which pleased Francis himself—the Franciscans continue to be omnipresent in ministering to the sick and in living among the poor today.

A Woman's Place?

Clare di Favarone was a great supporter and friend of Francis. In fact, her own efforts to feed the lepers living in the hills surrounding Assisi were a significant influence on Francis's own conversion. She yearned to live among the poor as Francis did. While the social pressures raised against Francis were enormous, those against a single woman of marrying age living this way proved to be insurmountable. Yet, with Francis's help, she appealed to the pope to found a cloistered order of religious women who would come to be known as the Poor Clares. Other young women joined Clare in dedicating themselves to lives of prayer and simplicity. Their primary aim was to support the efforts of the nascent Franciscan brothers in their apostolate to the poor. What was particularly unique about Clare's group, and it was noted by Pope Innoncent III himself, was their commitment to live in solidarity with the poor outside the walls of the cloister through their strict vow of poverty. (This is an ethic that is also very much at the heart of the spirituality of the religious order founded by Mother Teresa in modern times.)

There is a story about Clare that captures well her uncompromising commitment to service, which is at the heart of mendicant spirituality. Some of the women in ministry with Clare did not take the strict vows of cloistered community living, so that they would be permitted to leave the convent located next to the Church of San Damiano (which Clare and Francis together had rebuilt). Since shoes were a luxury not available to the poor, these women too would make their journeys through the muddy and garbage-strewn streets of Assisi barefoot. As Jesus did for his friends at the Last Supper (John 13:1–20), Clare would wash the feet of the returning workers herself whenever possible.

In a touching and fitting conclusion to their ministries, Francis spent the last couple of years of his life under the care of Clare and the sisters. Clare continued to insist on the unadulterated commitment to poverty and the poor, even in the face of efforts to expand the land and wealth of her order by Pope Gregory IX , for the rest of her life.

The Great Divide

The success of the Franciscans and Poor Clares inspired the growth and development of other mendicant religious orders, in particular the Carmelites, Augustinians, and the Dominicans. Dominic de Guzman, the founder of the Domincians, honored the spirit of the mendicant ideal but saw another pressing need among the common people. For centuries after the collapse of the Roman Empire, the vast majority of men and women in Europe received little if any organized education. Women were taught to perform the specific skills necessary to maintain a home and care for children, and some men were trained with the skills necessary to work at a particular craft through the guild system. Opportunities for any in-depth understanding of the natural world or of the Christian faith were severely limited.

Those beautiful stained-glass windows of the medieval cathedrals that we continue to admire today for their color and artistic achievement actually were created for pastoral reasons. The vast majority of the faithful were illiterate and therefore could not read the words of Scripture themselves. Keeping in mind the words of Paul that ignorance of Scripture is ignorance of Christ, the architects, builders, and bishops who oversaw the construction of the cathedrals used the medium of stained glass to tell the stories of the Bible and of the holy women and men the Church had canonized as saints. The colorful stories in glass, together with the transcendent beauty of the cathedral itself, gave the faithful who assembled there each Sunday the experience of being transported from the drab and harsh conditions that characterized their everyday lives into a foretaste of God's kingdom in all its fullness.

The downside of this situation, however, was that the strong sense of solidarity that existed in the early Christian Churches when the presiders, deacons, and deaconesses lived with and worked with the people they served on a daily basis was lost. Now that only the privileged few bishops and educated clergy could read and write, the written expressions of the Christian faith were understandable to only a few. And as meaningful catechesis was lost, so was an understanding of essential Christian beliefs and practices among the people.

This growing disconnect between hierarchy and laity was clearly manifested in the "source and summit" of Christian belief, the celebration of the Eucharist. By the thirteenth century, the faithful who assembled each Sunday had little understanding of the Latin language in which the Mass was celebrated or the obscure gestures and actions of a priest who stood far away, with his back to the people, often wreathed by a cloud of incense. (The magician's term "hocus pocus" originated in this inability to make sense of the Latin prayers recited at the altar. In this case, the words *Hoc est Corpus*, meaning "This is my body," were the source.) When it came time for Holy Communion, few felt worthy to receive the Body and Blood of Christ. Eucharistic adoration, intended as a secondary devotion, took the place of directly receiving the Eucharist for most Catholics.

The closer we look at this great divide, the more we can see the sense in the comment made by a number of historians. For many people in Western Europe, Christianity in the medieval period was a thin veneer over deep-seated and widely varying pagan customs and beliefs. A good example is the devotions to particular saints that date back to the days of the first martyrs in the Church. During the Middle Ages it became all too common for these devotions, referred to collectively as the "cult of the saints," to devolve from meditations on the lessons in discipleship offered by the life of a particular saint into obsessions with relics connected with the saint or images of the saint that were rumored to have miraculous powers. (Geoffrey Chaucer offers some colorful insights into the darker side of the cult of the saints in *Canterbury Tales*.)

Lack of Catechesis

Dominic de Guzman recognized that this vast "disconnect" was the result of a lack of good catechesis. He further understood that the dearth of good teaching was just as great a poverty as the material poverty of the age. With the rise of towns and a nascent middle class in many places, came both a hunger among the laity to learn more and the creation of a merchant class with the means to support a more widespread catechetical ministry in the Church. Further hastening the movement of the Spirit for Dominic and the members of his order was the rise of heresies within the Church that were often a direct result of this widespread ignorance of true Christian teaching. Most particularly, Dominic faced the challenge of the Albigensians.

The Albigensian heresy, so called because the movement centered around the city of Albi in southern France, was the product of a very old heresy and a genuine desire for a wide-ranging reform of the corrupt hierarchy of the Church. The example given at the beginning of this chapter, as well as the story of the wealthy French nobleman who purchased the office of archbishop for his eleven-year-old son, suggest that too often the magisterium of the Church had ceased to listen to the promptings of the Holy Spirit.

Unfortunately in the case of the Albigensians, this reforming zeal was coupled with a variation of Gnosticism, the heretical belief that Jesus could not have been fully human because flesh is inherently corrupt. From a Gnostic point of view, Jesus' greatness is in his possession of a special knowledge, or "gnosis" that revealed to him the true nature of God and the universe. Salvation, therefore, is not universal, and not mediated through the cross, but rather is limited to those few individuals who possess the same gnosis that Jesus did, and thus can fully understand his words. Dominic saw the handwriting on the wall as the size of the Albigensian movement and the determination of Church leadership to eliminate the threat made conflict inevitable.

In an effort to combat the heresy through education and not violent confrontation, Dominic and members of his order went from village to village, preaching and teaching the basics of the Christian faith, subsisting, as the Franciscans did, only on the generosity of the people of that particular region. Eventually, the hierarchy of the Church recognized the effectiveness of the Dominican ministry and incorporated the Dominicans, as well as some of the Franciscans, into the developing institutions of higher learning sponsored by the Church. Ironically, the Dominicans sometimes found themselves in the role of the Grand Inquisitors (a Church office established to root out heresy) during the time of the infamous Inquisition. (We will take a closer look at the Inquisition and at the bloody suppression of the Albigensian heresy in Chapter Seven.)

The "Dumb Ox" Speaks

A most significant result of the trends described so far in this chapter was the development of the great universities of Europe in the twelfth and thirteenth centuries. Originally cathedral schools founded to educate the clergy, these institutions of higher learning expanded their curricula beyond philosophy and theology into the arts and sciences. As the work of the ancients were rediscovered, the universities became places were they could be explored in depth. Many of the renowned universities of Europe today (Oxford, Bologna, Florence, Paris, and Cologne, for example) trace their origins to this time period. The need for qualified teachers was great, and time and time again the pope turned to the Dominicans and Franciscans to help staff them.

The names of some of the great teachers of this era—Anselm, considered the founder of Scholasticism; the brilliant Franciscan named Bonaventure; Peter Lombard; and Albert Magnus—are still recognized today and honored by the Church. But the one who stands in front of them all is Thomas Aquinas (1225–74) whose dictum of "faith seeking understanding" built on and completed the work of the scholastic scholars who preceded him. Thomas proved once and for all that divine revelation and human reason are not bitter enemies but two unique gifts from the same gracious God. In working out his synthesis between the best in human thought—personified in the works of the Greek philosopher Aristotle—and the truths of divine revelation, Thomas, fully grounded in the Christian belief in the Incarnation, gave a massive body blow to the Gnostic beliefs that the material world ought to be looked upon with contempt and rejected by "the saved."

Thomas of Aquinas wrote enough books and letters to fill a library, including a great defense of Christianity entitled the *Summa Contra Gentiles*. His masterpiece is the *Summa Theologica*, a compendium of questions, thesis, and antithesis that explore every conceivable topic in the Christian theology and philosophy of the day. Here's a sample from the *Summa* that illustrates Thomas's attempt to show the natural harmony between faith and reason, often referred to as the scholastic method. It concerns the question of whether or not God exists:

Objection 1: It seems that God does not exist, because if one of two contraries be infinite, the other would be altogether destroyed....If, therefore, God existed, there would be no evil discoverable; but there is evil in the world.

On the contrary, it is said in the person of God: *I am Who am* (Exodus 3:14).

I answer that, The existence of God can be proved in five ways....

He then proceeds to explain five proofs of God's existence. Each one of which is a logical deduction based on principles of reason and evidence of the five senses. For example, he argues:

> The third way....We find in nature things that could either exist or not exist....It is impossible for these always to exist, for that which can one day cease to exist must at some time have not existed...therefore, if at one time nothing was in existence, it would have been impossible for anything to have begun to exist; and thus even now nothing would be in existence—which is absurd. Therefore, not all beings are merely possible, but there must exist something the existence of which is necessary....This all men speak of as God.

The small excerpt here cannot do full justice to the integrity, depth, and breadth of Thomas's intellect. What is clear even from this small sample, however, is the remarkable synthesis Thomas and the scholastics in general were able to achieve. Thomas' belief in God is founded in a faith experience, but he uses the fullness of the gifts of reason God has given him to probe and question and deepen his understanding of the mystery that grounds his being. The Gnostic contempt for the material world poisoned the well of genuine Christian spirituality, often masquerading as orthodoxy. The life and writings of Thomas Aquinas in their own way witness to the awesome truth of the Incarnation—that through Jesus the goodness of creation and of the spirit are forever united and give glory to God.

Thomas's efforts to bring together the best of theology and philosophy known to the Western world was not universally well received during his lifetime. Many felt that Christian thinkers had no business being involved with pagan philosophers such as Aristotle. It would take more than a century for Thomas to be canonized as a saint and given the title he so richly deserved: Doctor of the Church. The scholastic method that Thomas perfected remained the dominant approach to Catholic theology well into the twentieth century.

The Mystics

Flowering side by side with the new mendicant orders was the tradition of mysticism in the West. Mysticism can be defined as attempts to encounter the mystery of God in a more direct way not mediated by the emotions or the intellect. The anonymous author of *The Cloud of Unknowing*, the classic text exploring the dynamic of the mystical experience, wrote during this era that the mystical experience occurs after an individual has reached a level of intimacy with God in prayer in which words fail and emotions are transcended. Ironically, this transformation in which the individual is objectively becoming more aware of the intimate presence of God subjectively feels like a tremendous absence. During this "dark night of the soul," as a later mystic, Saint John of the Cross, called it, the contemplative may be close to despair with feelings of abandonment and frustration at having lost the ability to pray. What is really happening, however, is just the opposite, and eventually the mystic's understanding and experience of God is completely transformed.

Generally speaking, such a progression in the spiritual life requires a great deal of time and access to solitude and silence. It is not surprising, therefore, that the mystical tradition in the Eastern Church developed centuries earlier than in the West, concurrent with the explosive growth of monastic living there in the early centuries of Church history. It is a primary reason, as mentioned in the last chapter, that the understanding of faith as an ongoing journey into the mystery of God has traditionally been so much more a part of Eastern Christian spirituality than Western spirituality. In the centuries following the collapse of Charlemagne's empire, however, the West began to catch up.

Hildegard and Julian

Two of the great mystics whose lives mark the beginning and the end of this medieval era of rebuilding the Church are Hildegard of Bingen (1098–1179) and Julian of Norwich (1342–1416). Both women enjoyed long lives and exerted tremendous influences through the power of their holiness and intelligence. Both contributed to the development of lay spirituality in the Church. At times their intense devotions and attempts to live out their experiences of Christ's limitless love, which is at the base of any authentic mystical experience, put them in conflict with the ecclesiastical powers of their times.

Hildegard became a prioress of a convent operating according to the Rule of Benedict in the Rhineland when she was in her thirties. From childhood on, she had experienced intense spiritual visions that "burned her soul," as she once said to her confessor, Bernard of Clairvaux. She began writing down the visions as best she could ten years later. Eventually, she combined her writings in what would become known as her major work, *Scito via Domini* (*Know the Ways of the Lord*). Her mystical experiences came to the attention of Pope Eugenius III, who, finding nothing in them in contradiction to the essential teachings of the Christian faith, gave Hildegard the Church's blessing.

Not every bishop was quite so magnanimous. When Hildegard allowed a young man, who had been excommunicated from the Church, to be buried in the hallowed grounds of the convent, the local bishop was furious. He demanded that the corpse be removed from sacred ground. Hildegard tried impassioned reason based on their mutual belief in the generous forgiveness of God. When that failed to warm the bishop's heart, she simply had all evidence of the grave removed so the body could never be found! (Saints may have their imaginations in the kingdom of God but their feet are always firmly planted on earth!)

The particulars of the life of Julian of Norwich are more obscure. The dates of her birth and death are only approximations based on historical inferences. Most of what is known about her is based on the two versions of her reflections on her mystical experiences, most of which centered around the Passion of Jesus. Julian spent a great part of her adult life as an anchoress, a hermit who lived in a walled enclosure, known as an anchorhold, attached to a church. (Men were called "anchorites.") The anchoress's days were spent in a combination of prayer and ministry, which consisted of offering spiritual direction to all those who might come by from the surrounding villages seeking guidance. The visitor would speak to the anchoress through a window that opened up either onto the street or a vestibule.

Unimaginable Love and Mercy

Concerning her own mystical experiences, Julian wrote that these intimate encounters with God were only meaningful to the extent they moved the mystic to a greater understanding of the unimaginable love and mercy God bestows on human beings through Jesus. While the scholastics were hammering in more explicit terms the logical deductions grounded in that same unconditional love and mercy of God, the anchoress reached out to the hearts of the common people for whom much of the work of the scholastics was inaccessible. Whatever the starting point, however, the truth of the mystic and the scholar came together in the person of Jesus Christ.

In her book on the life and theology of Julian of Norwich, Grace Jantzen illustrates the contrast of the two approaches to the essential Christian belief in the Trinity. During the course of his Trinitarian proofs in the *Summa*, Thomas Aquinas says the following:

> We must consequently admit that spiration belongs to the person of the Father and to the person of the Son, inasmuch as it has on relative opposition either to paternity or to filiation; and consequently that procession belongs to the other person who is called the person of the Holy Ghost....Therefore only three persons exist in God, the Father, the Son, and the Holy Ghost. (*Summa Theologiae* as quoted in *Julian of Norwich: Mystic and Theologian*, p. 113)

Julian puts it this way:

> Our Father wills, our Mother (Christ) works, our good Lord the Holy Spirit confirms. And therefore it is our part to love our God in whom we have our being, reverently thanking and praising him for our creation, mightily praying to our Mother for mercy and pity, and to our Lord the Holy Spirit for help and grace. For in these three is all our life.

Often the Middle Ages have been trumpeted as the "golden age" of the Catholic Church. Such an assumption seems hard to understand at first. It's hard to imagine a kingdom of God replete with bloody crusades, the torturing and burning of heretics, all-too-worldly leaders, and a great divide between clergy and laity, both in catechesis and the celebration of the Eucharist. And yet, there is a grain of truth to this claim.

For like the glorious Gothic cathedrals whose steeples rose into the sky and whose glass and stone infused the sacred space with a palpable sense of God's presence, so the three centuries following the turn of the first millennium were a time during which three vital streams of Catholic spirituality came together. The radical commitment to the poor and oppressed of the mendicants, the uncompromising intellectual integrity and faith of the scholastics, and the transcendent experience of the mystics all flowed together in a river of God's grace that filled the hearts and minds of the people of God in powerful and glorious ways.

The Revival of the Papacy

The monastic tradition that began in the East in the fourth century, and that was established through the Benedictine Rule in the West several centuries later, bore fruit in unexpected ways. The monasteries in the remote portions of northern Europe, as well as in the deserts of the Middle East, became repositories of the writings of the ancient world and the early Church, as barbarian tribes and Muslim invaders brought the ancient world to an end. Often the monastery or convent became a place of refuge for the populace in times of war or famine or illness. And because they were independent and subject only to the authority of the abbot or the prioress, the monasteries and convents were spared much of the corruption and chaos that engulfed Western Europe in the ninth and tenth centuries. They became centers for reform on a number of occasions.

Almost contemporaneous with the collapse of Charlemagne's empire, was the rise of the monastic community at Cluny, France. It was Cluny that supplied some of the most devoted and honest men to the leadership of the Church during a period that is widely acknowledged as the low point of the papacy. As the vitality of the Clunaic reform began to subside, the torch was passed to such notables as Bernard of Clairvaux and the order of Cistercian monks he founded in 1098.

This force of renewal, coupled with the efforts of such notably courageous and enlightened bishops as Thomas à Becket and propelled by the spiritual revolution happening among the people, enabled the papacy to respond to the urgent call of the Spirit and purge itself of the rapacious thugs who had infested it. In the eleventh and twelfth centuries, popes whose power was rooted in faith and not wealth or position stood up to the parade of petty princes and power-hungry kings who sought to control the temporal power of the Church to advance their own agendas. Most notable is the case of Pope Gregory VII, who excommunicated King Henry IV in 1076 in an effort to reassert the Church's right to appoint its own bishops without interference from the State. (This ongoing struggle between Church and state is known as the "lay investiture crisis.") The story goes that the pope would not lift the excommunication against the king, and by extension his people, until Henry stood barefoot in the snow for three days outside of Gregory's northern Italian castle in Canossa. By the end of the eleventh century, the prestige and influence of the papacy had been restored to the point that Pope Urban II was able to marshal the wealth and manpower of Western Europe to create an army of Crusaders bound for Jerusalem. (For a fuller discussion of the Crusades, see Chapter Seven.)

Strong popes began reforms within the Church as well. In 1075, Gregory VII declared celibacy a requirement for ordination to the priesthood and took steps to enforce the edict in deed as well as word. While celibacy was not a requirement for the priesthood in the first millennium of Church history (the Scriptures mention that Peter had a mother-in-law, for example), it had always been upheld as a powerful witness to the ministers' commitment to God and to the people if it was genuinely and freely embraced. It was all too common, however, by the eleventh century for a cleric to hypocritically profess the holiness of a celibate vocation while being involved with a mistress. Gregory's edict had another more practical motivation as well. It would settle the bothersome issue of what to do about the inheritance of Church lands if a priest or bishop had children!

By the time of Pope Innocent III (1198–1216), the papacy had reached a level of power and influence across Europe, both in secular matters and spiritual matters, that it would never reach again. Not only had the forces of lay investiture been beaten back for a time, but the right of the pope to *appoint* the bishops of other dioceses—as opposed to the right of the community to select its own bishop as was true in the early Church—had now been firmly established as the norm. Innocent's decision to recognize the first mendicant religious orders suggests that the harmony the Holy Spirit always motivates the Church to seek (between the teachings of the magisterium and the beliefs and practices of the people) was manifested to a significant extent in the waning days of the medieval period. It was a tangible expression of the *sensus fidei* achieved just as the Church faced the death of one world and the calamitous birth of another. Meeting the spiritual needs of the modern era would require the Church to begin a fundamental change of mindset not seen since the days of the first apostolic generation.

For Thought and Discussion

1) After reading this chapter, what do you think are the chief reasons for the decline in the leadership of the Church in the ninth and tenth centuries?

2) In what ways was the approach of the mendicants different than earlier attempts to meet the needs of the poor? How does the Church meet these needs today?

3) How were the approaches of Clare and Francis of Assisi different from Dominic de Guzman's approach? How were they similar? What do you think are the advantages and disadvantages of each?

4) Do you think that faith and reason complement one another in modern religious beliefs and practices? Why or why not?

5) In what ways do you think Thomas, Hildegard of Bingen, and Julian of Norwich challenged the Church to "change its mind" during the medieval period?

6) Compare and contrast the ways in which the scholastics expressed their understanding of the fundamental truths of Catholic Christianity with the ways of the mystics. What do you think are the advantages of each approach?

7) Would you characterize the Middle Ages as the "golden age" of the Church? Why or why not?

8) Discuss the relationship between the magisterium and the faithful in the formation of the *sensus fidei* of this era.

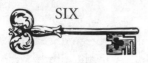

SIX

Reformation

> For this authority, though given to a man and exercised by a man, is not human, but rather divine....Furthermore, we declare, state, define, and pronounce that it is altogether necessary to salvation for every human creature to be subject to the Roman pontiff.

These words, written in 1296 by Pope Boniface VIII in his encyclical *Unam Sanctam*, succinctly capture the awe with which the papacy was viewed by the populace—and by the popes themselves—during the time commonly referred to as the High Middle Ages. They express the basis of the "two swords" theory of church-state relationships: while the responsibilities of bishop and secular ruler are distinct, both are ordained by God to advance the establishment of God's kingdom on earth. The king, therefore, is ultimately responsible to the chief of all bishops, the Bishop of Rome.

Boniface's words also mark the beginning of the collapse of Christendom. In 1303, Boniface was arrested by King Philip IV of France, a monarch who did not share the pontiff's idea of the proper church-state relationship. The pope's fate foreshadowed the history of the Church over the next two centuries, culminating in the events of the Protestant Reformation. Forces within and outside the Church would once and for all shatter the image of the Church as a secular and spiritual power rooted in the time of Emperor Constantine and developed during the subsequent collapse of the Roman Empire in the West. What emerged from this crisis was the paradox of a Church that could articulate every "jot and tittle" of its doctrines and dogmas but was unable to grasp the fundamental transformation in its own identity.

Catherine of Siena

Catherine of Siena (1347–80) was an extraordinary woman in a number of ways. The youngest of twenty-five children born to Jacopo and Monna Lapa Benincasa, Catherine learned to read and write in a time when illiteracy was widespread among men and basically a given among women whose identities were firmly grounded in the tasks of maintaining the home. Catherine was never one to follow the norms of her times, however; at age sixteen she entered religious life through her local chapter of the Dominican Third Order, and within a few years she was deeply immersed in works of charity among the poor and needy of Siena.

The same prejudices and suspicions that forced Clare into a cloistered life a hundred years before made life difficult for Catherine as well. As men and women began to seek her out for inspiration and spiritual counsel, her neighbors in Siena began to wonder out loud what Catherine might really be doing behind closed doors. (Mary Magdalene is the first in a long line of Christian women to have been labeled either a prostitute or witch for daring to go beyond the arbitrary boundaries of a patriarchal culture in order to follow Christ.) Yet Catherine persisted lovingly in the work of her ministry, distinguishing herself in a particular way during the outbreak of the bubonic plague that ravaged Seina in 1374.

Perhaps the necessity of learning how to speak kindly with those who had no kind words in return contributed to the reputation Catherine developed as a peacemaker and mediator. As time went by, Catherine became a confidant of popes and princes, her brilliant mind expressing itself through numerous letters and an outstanding work of theology and mysticism, *Divine Dialogue*. What Catherine saw most clearly was the dangerous state of affairs in the Church that existed in the late fourteenth century.

Pope Boniface VIII died soon after his arrest in 1303. King Philip then seized the opportunity. He knew that Rome was only a shadow of its former glory, a place of crumbling ruins and an impoverished population. Appealing particularly to the French bishops' nascent sense of nationalism, the king engineered the relocation of the papacy to a splendid new palace and court in Avignon. For the next seventy years, the southern coast of France became the residence of the popes.

Back to Rome

Catherine of Siena was able to articulate the frustration and anxiety many of the faithful were experiencing as a result of the Avignon papacy. Rome meant more to Catholics than the city itself. It was the See of Saint Peter and thus a symbol of the universal call to minister to the entire Church, a mantle one after another of his successors carried. In Rome, the pope spoke on behalf of the entire Church. In Avignon, he spoke on behalf of the French. It was inevitable that this perception of the pope as an agent of the French king, as well as the growing opulence of the papal court, would demean the papacy and the entire institutional Church in the eyes of many of the faithful.

After a series of fruitless appeals to the pope to return home, Catherine decided that desperate times called for desperate measures. Dispensing with correspondence, she made an arduous journey over land and sea from the town of Siena (located in the northern part of the Italian peninsula) to Avignon in 1376. She got right to the point in a meeting with Pope Gregory XI a few days after she arrived: "To the glory of Almighty God I am bound to say that I smelled the stink of the sins which flourish in the papal court while I was still at home in my own town more sharply than those who have practiced them, and do practice them, every day here" (quoted in *Women in Church History* by Joanne Turpin, p. 112).

The force of Catherine's words, personality, and sanctity did help persuade the pope to return to Rome. Unfortunately, the damage had already been done. To make matters much worse, whatever prestige Gregory XI had restored to the papacy by his return was quickly squandered after his death in 1378. During the next forty years, the Church endured the Great Western Schism as bishops deeply divided among themselves and often pressured by the political forces of the day broke into two factions, one supporting a pope in Rome and the other a pope in Avignon. The schism reached the depths of absurdity in the early 1400s when a bungled attempt by the council of Pisa to heal the split led to the election of yet a third pope! By the time Martin V was chosen as pope by the Council of Constance in 1417, the papacy, and for the most part the hierarchy of the Church in general, had lost its ability to be a moral and spiritual compass for the rest of the faithful.

God on Demand

This leadership was sorely needed as the great divide between the way the people of God expressed their faith and the true experience of discipleship became wider and wider. As was discussed in the last chapter, even during the so-called glory days of the twelfth and thirteenth centuries in the Roman Catholic Church, the majority of the faithful no longer understood what the celebration of the Eucharist really meant. Lacking this vital connection with the "source and summit" of the Christian faith meant that all other aspects of Christian life would in time become deformed as well.

From the beginning, the gospel proclamation is clear: "For God so loved the world that he sent his only Son, so that everyone who believes in him might not perish but may have eternal life" (John 3:16). This belief in the Incarnation (God as fully human in the person of Jesus of Nazareth) is the core belief of Christianity, the belief that gives Christianity its unique identity as a religion. Seen in the context of the Hebrew Scriptures, the Christian gospel is understood to be the extension of God's covenanted promise to Israel: "You will be my people and I will be your God." Through belief in Jesus Christ, we are caught up in a relationship with a God who wants to be known and loved by us.

We don't do good things, in other words, to earn God's love. It's only after we have begun to experience the unconditional love of God through Christ that we really become able to do good things. Paul puts it this way: "Indeed, rarely will anyone die for a righteous person— though perhaps for a good person someone might actually dare to die. But God proves his love for us in that while we still were sinners Christ died for us" (Romans 5:7–8). What a stark contrast this proclamation is to the oppressive belief that God must be appeased through sacrifice, ritual, and human efforts, a belief that has formed the superstructure of religious belief throughout human history.

vending machine
1500

Sadly, by the fourteenth century this tendency toward appeasement had deeply distorted the rituals, beliefs, and practices of the Church. For too many clerics and lay people alike, the Christian religion had become mechanical. God was perceived somewhat like the owner of a giant vending machine (the Church) that dispensed grace (God's love) through the pope and the bishops, only after the proper coins (prayers, fasting, penance, etc.) had been inserted. Particular expressions of this "vending machine" mentality were manifold.

For example, consider the widespread veneration of relics (actual physical remains of the canonized saints or things associated with particular saints). By the fifteenth century, the buying and selling of relics had been a big business for a long time. Beliefs abounded that close contact with such sacred items would yield tremendous spiritual benefits. In 1517, the year that Martin Luther posted his ninety-five theses on the door of the Wittenberg cathedral, the Archbishop Albert of Mainz boasted of a collection of 9,000 relics, including "whole bodies of saints, a bone of Isaac, manna from the wilderness, a bit of Moses' burning bush, a jar from Cana (with actual wine in it), a bit of the crown of thorns, and one of the stones that killed St. Stephen" (Paul Johnson, *A History of Christianity*, p. 281).

Crusaders marched off to battle, confident that by engaging in armed conflict with the Muslim infidels, any number of sins committed during their lifetime would be remitted. Pilgrimages to various places, such as the shrine of St. James in Spain or that of Thomas à Becket in England, were tremendously popular, in part for the special remission of sin granted by the pope to any Catholic who made the journey. Even the vibrant and colorful cult of the saints, by means of which thousands of the faithful made meaningful spiritual connections with Christ through devotion to saintly intermediaries, had a dark underside. Sometimes particular prayers or statues were imbued with a kind of magic in the minds of the faithful; because of this, it was believed that the saint could be manipulated to grant the petitioner whatever he or she desired.

Indulgences

All of these expressions of vending-machine Christianity were eclipsed, however, by the scandalous practices involving the buying and selling of indulgences in the fifteenth and early sixteenth centuries. Ironically, the concept of an indulgence is grounded in that same Christian experience of the unconditional love of God we have just explored. God's grace, poured out in its fullness through Jesus Christ, is like a waterfall, continually showering the human race. God's intent, implicit in the second creation story told in Genesis 2:3 (note the presence of the tree of eternal life) and made explicit in the Resurrection, is for human beings to enter into this covenanted relationship of love for all eternity. To be fully human, therefore, is to have crossed from death to life through Christ and to live in eternal and perfect communion with God and with the other members of the "Church in Perfection," the saints in heaven.

Our expressed belief conveyed in the Nicene Creed through the phrase "the communion of saints" is that the Church exists simultaneously in three distinct but united dimensions. The visible Church encompasses those of us bound in mortal flesh who journey together on pilgrimage, constantly being drawn by God's grace into repentance and renewal and ever deeper union with Christ. Those souls making up the "Church in Perfection" described above—a few declared to be saints through the process of canonization but most known only by God and by those whose lives they touched while on pilgrimage—now possess a broader vision and fuller sanctity. No longer seeing by "faith but by sight" as Paul says, they are able to unite their prayers with our own and to amplify them before God.

This glorious communion and celebration of the love of God freely poured down upon all of God's children means that, in some mysterious way—and that phrasing is important—the community of believers through Christ can petition God to "direct" grace toward members of the community who are in particular need, especially because of the effects of sin. God's generosity is such that in response to our petitions, God grants "indulgences," roughly speaking, extra dollops of grace as needed. (It's important to note here that even before we become aware of our needs and the needs of the community, God already knows them, and grants us the grace which enables us to pray. Or, as Paul says, the Holy Spirit prays within us.)

Over the centuries, the belief developed in the Catholic Church that some souls in making the transition from Pilgrimage to Perfection needed to pass through a kind of a purification or purgation (the origin of the word "purgatory"). Those individuals making up the "Church in Purgation," the third dimension, could be aided by this same glorious communion described above through the prayers in word and action of those of us still on pilgrimage. In 1476, Pope Sixtus IV made explicit the connection that many of the faithful had already made in practice between the belief in the communion of saints, indulgences, and purgatory by granting particular indulgences for prayers and for charitable actions made on behalf of the souls in purgatory.

The Death Spiral

How an expression of God's unconditional love and the enduring nature of Christian community became the horrid mess that sparked the Protestant Reformation involves a combination of poor theology, bad habits, and greed. It's important to remember that no Christian Church—either Protestant or Roman Catholic or Eastern Orthodox—teaches that God's grace through indulgences or any other practices can be "earned." Just as the members of any loving family do, we pray and make sacrifices and repent for the sake of one another, not to earn the other's love, but *because* we are caught up in relationship of love. It is God's love and faithfulness that brings us into eternal communion with God and one another, but that love and faithfulness cries out to be incarnated in the real fabric of our lives as individual disciples and as a community.

As the late Middle Ages progressed, however, an unholy synthesis developed. An inadequate understanding of purgatory as some sort of a non-permanent place of torment embedded itself in the Catholic imagination. The mechanical understanding of Christianity already described distorted the commission of Jesus to Peter recorded in the gospel of Matthew: "Whatever you bind on earth will be bound in heaven, and whatever you loose on earth will be loosed in heaven" (16:19). Rather than seeing themselves as the guides who were to help the faithful recognize the waterfall of grace drenching them, and to help them enter more deeply into it, the magisterium of the Church began to see itself as the *very pipes* through which that grace would be dispensed. (Reread the beginning of this chapter for a good example of this mindset.) Thus the pope had the authority to turn on the spigot or to turn it off and to set up particular means by which the faithful could access God's grace.

What a far cry this was from the point Jesus makes in the gospels in the story of the cleansing of the temple! To make matters much worse than they might otherwise have been, the long-term effect of the Avignon papacy and Great Schism was a papacy that had developed a keen taste for wealth and power and indifference toward the spiritual life. Wealthy families like the Medicis and Borgias vied with one another during the times of the Renaissance papacy—often through illicit means—to ensure that a family member gained the papal throne. Generally speaking, the lives of the Renaissance popes resembled the lives of any other Italian nobles of the period, including ostentatious wealth and an abundance of courtiers and mistresses. (I used to help my students remember the name of Alexander VI, for example, by remarking to them that he had fathered six illegitimate children!)

While this worldly immersion of the Renaissance popes did produce some of the greatest works of Western art (remember, this is the age of Leonardo DaVinci, Michelangelo, and Raphael), it had a deadening effect on the spiritual life of the Church. Most importantly for our understanding of what happened next, this desire to express the glory of the Church through accumulating the riches of the world, culminating in the building of a brand new St. Peter's basilica, meant that the popes needed money and lots of it.

By 1517, the "perfect storm" was already raging. Individuals desperate to relieve the perceived torments of loved ones in purgatory eagerly sought papal indulgences that might shorten their stay. The demand for indulgences, combined with the financial pressures described above, motivated the popes to "simplify" the means by which indulgences might be granted. Rather than performing acts of charity themselves, wealthy individuals could pay others to perform them on their behalf, or contribute sums to particular pet projects of the bishop or pope.

Gradually, even this intermediary step disappeared and those who had the means could purchase indulgences for the remission of punishment due to sin from Church-sanctioned pardoners, who were essentially medieval insurance salesmen. Pardoners traveled from town to town as full-service merchants of vending-machine Christianity, equipped with "authentic" relics for sale as well as particular indulgences. (See Chaucer's *Canterbury Tales* for a depiction of a pardoner in all his glory.) Some pardoners, such as Johann Tetzel, even had their own jingles: "When a coin in the coffer sings, a soul from purgatory springs!"

A Time of Revolution *Reformation*   *Luther 95 theses*

When Martin Luther, an Augustinian monk, posted his ninety-five theses—that is, topics for debate—on the door of the Wittenberg
Cathedral in Germany, he was following the procedure of any scholar
who wished to introduce topics for discussion at the colleges always
connected with the important churches of Europe. A number of these
debate topics focused on the abuses associated with the way in which
the Church was meting out indulgences. Luther's concerns were by no
means radical; many within the Church—clerics, theologians, and
laity—were deeply troubled by what was happening. In fact, this fundamental rebellion against vending-machine Christianity had roots
going back at least two centuries.

But Luther's critique had two powerful forces behind it that former
protests lacked. One was the printing press, invented in 1450, which
enabled Luther and other Protestant reformers to disperse their ideas to
a much wider audience then ever before possible. The other shows its
origins in the behavior of Philip IV toward Pope Boniface VIII. As the
nation-states of Europe began to emerge, the average European began to
see himself or herself less as a subject of Christendom and more as a citizen of a particular nation or province. Ambitious princes and kings
wishing to advance their own political agendas both encouraged this
change and were emboldened by it to defy papal temporal authority,
and sometimes spiritual authority as well. (In their courageous opposition to Henry VIII's decision to declare himself the supreme head of the
English Church in 1534, bishop John Fisher and statesman Thomas
More gave powerful witness to how a Spirit-led *sensus fidei* can manifest
itself among clergy and laity regardless of external pressures to suppress
it. Together they stood for a wider vision of Church; together they were
imprisoned in the Tower of London; together through martyrdom they
now rejoice within the communion of saints.)

Even had the papacy been at the top of its game, taming the firestorm
that began as Luther's ideas received wider dissemination would have
been a Herculean task. But the last of the Renaissance popes, Leo X, was
not competent to comprehend this "squabble among monks," much less
address the fundamental spiritual crisis behind it. Attempts were made
to force Luther to recant, all of which failed, and in 1521 at the Diet of
Worms Luther was officially declared a heretic and excommunicated.

Excommunication at a time when the Church wielded temporal as well as spiritual power meant that Luther was now an outlaw as well.

Sensing an opportunity to claim his independence from both the Church and the Holy Roman Empire, Frederick of Saxony staged a "kidnapping" of Luther in order to get him safely into his castle at Wartburg. From the security of this exile in the German lands, Luther wrote voluminously and began to lay down the basic principles of Protestant theology. Among his fundamental ideas was the importance of rejecting the centuries of doctrines and rituals that had obscured the message of the Scriptures and returning to prayerful reading of and meditation on the texts themselves (*Sola Scriptura*). Luther rejected the vending-machine approach to Christian discipleship by insisting on the "priesthood of the people," the idea that no human being required a mediator in order to reach God, but could do so personally through Jesus.

Luther's ideas spread through northern Europe like wildfire. By 1526, there were enough followers of Luther in the German National Assembly that they had been given a new name. That title of "Protestant" was not so much a religious designation as an indication of their constant opposition to policies of the Catholic emperor. When the Augsburg Confession was completed by Luther's brilliant disciple Philip Melancthon in 1530, Lutheranism was established as a distinct Christian Church with its own particular theology.

Protestantism Goes International

Luther did not originally intend to found a new church but was carried away by events. John Calvin (1509–64) did. Calvin was studying in Paris in the early 1530s when he first came across Luther's writings and was inspired by them. He saw in Luther's work the basis for an entirely new way to construct a Christian Church. "New" is a relative term here; Calvin's decentralized view of independent small congregations led by bodies of "elders" (*presbyteroi* in Greek) and served by deacons very much resembled the size and shape of the earliest Christian Churches in the Greco-Roman world.

Whereas those early churches were independent from and sometimes in opposition to the civil authorities of the Roman Empire, however, Calvin's plan was to create a theocracy in which the religious commandments of the faith would also function as the legal code for the state.

(The current Muslim theocracy in Iran is a helpful example in understanding what Calvin had in mind.) Ironically, this kind of governance, which Calvin implemented in Geneva, Switzerland, went far beyond what the most autocratic bishops in Europe attempted to do. Even Boniface VIII saw the laws of Church and state as distinctly separate entitites. Eventually the particular kind of theocracy Calvin had in mind was rejected by most Protestant congregations—the Puritans of the Massachusetts Bay colony in the seventeenth century are a notable exception—but the method of creating a Church outlined by Calvin proved to be quite portable and allowed Protestantism to become an international religion.

Calvin's other lasting legacy is his massive treatise on Christian theology, entitled *The Institutes of the Christian Religion*. Unlike Luther's writings, Calvin's developed a theology in direct contradiction to Catholic doctrine on several fundamental points. He explicitly denied the Real Presence in the Eucharist, asserting that the Christ is not present in the bread and wine but only in heaven. His doctrine of predestination presents a dark view of humanity, focusing mainly on the fallen state of humankind because of original sin and much less on the fundamental sacredness of the human person that is basic to both the Hebrew Scriptures (see Genesis 1:27) and the Christian belief in the Incarnation.

Such an emphasis made it hard for Calvin to see how human beings could be saved at all. In fact, he believed that most are not saved. God's graciousness has raised some members of depraved humanity destined for damnation onto the level of "the elect" destined for eternal salvation. The catch was Calvin's insistence that it was impossible to know for certain during earthly life whether or not you were a member of the elect. However, those living an industrious, virtuous Christian life (as Calvin conceived it, anyway) would certainly seem to be bearing the marks of the elect.

While you might think at first glance that Calvin's theology of salvation would be repulsive to most Christians, consider the nature of vending-machine Christianity from the point of view of the common people. Implicit in Calvin's theology is the belief that salvation has nothing to do with the whim of a powerful bishop or the pope himself. Having the money and influence to gain indulgences no longer mattered; any virtuous person might have a shot at salvation. This idea was a breath of fresh air to thousands of Christians who found the ways of the hierarchy of the Catholic Church to be increasingly hard to understand.

The Fantastic Four

Amid the chaos, excommunications, and impending violence of the Protestant Reformation, there were some within the Roman Catholic Church who attempted genuine reform. Four notables are Erasmus (1464–1536), Teresa of Avila (1515–82), John of the Cross (1542–91), and Ignatius of Loyola (1542–91). In distinctly different ways, Erasmus the scholar, Teresa and John the mystics, and Ignatius the soldier helped lay the groundwork that would point the Church into the future.

Erasmus was as scandalized by vending-machine Christianity as was Luther: "Perhaps thou believest that all thy sins are washed away with a little paper, a sealed parchment, with the gift of a little money, or some wax image, with a little pilgrimage. Thou art utterly deceived." He also recognized that genuine reform was impossible without a thorough reorientation of the Church back toward the Scriptures.

What ultimately led to a bitter divide between Eramus and Luther, however, was Erasmus's conviction that the Church could change its mind if the community were truly open to the Holy Spirit and thus reform *within* the Church was possible, but in God's time. "Vigorous minds will not suffer compulsion," he wrote sometime after Luther's excommunication. "To exercise compulsion is typical of tyrants, to suffer it, typical of asses" (quotes found in *A History of Christianity* by Paul Johnson, pp. 274–76). For a time Erasmus's writings evoked much sympathy among Roman Catholics, but as attitudes hardened and ground for compromise evaporated in the 1530s and 1540s much of his work was dismissed as too conciliatory to the Protestant heretics. Yet Erasmus laid down the basic ideals that would characterize authentic reform of the Church in the centuries to come.

Teresa of Avila, along with Catherine of Siena and Thérèse of Lisieux are the only women ever to be declared Doctors of the Church. Teresa entered the Carmelite order when she was twenty-one years old. Her vivacious personality and good looks were not a natural fit with the rigors and routines of cloistered living and Teresa seems to have struggled greatly in finding her way. This struggle bore much fruit, however, as she gradually discovered over the next twenty years that her vocation was much like those of Francis and Clare of Assisi—to return the Carmelite order to its mendicant roots. In her day, the convent seemed to be a way to give a comfortable living to unmarried young women of the nobility.

Her attempts at reform were not well received in this era of the Renaissance papacy, however. Eventually, she left the convent in which she had spent more than two decades in order to found a new order of Discalced ("barefoot") Carmelites. As she revealed in her masterpiece of theology and mysticism, *The Interior Castle*, Teresa's intense spiritual experiences of the love of Jesus transformed her and steeled her in her determination to love the poor with that same passionate intensity that Jesus loved her.

Spanish Revival

Teresa's struggles to reform the Carmelites are poignantly captured in her reflection that "the worst thing is when good people misunderstand." Yet she did find some allies along the way as her efforts were joined by those of other men and women of good will in leading a revitalization of the Church. Cardinal Ximenes was a great leader of the Catholic reformation in Spain, for example. She had no greater ally, however, than the young Carmelite friar half her age known to us as John of the Cross.

Along with Teresa's own work, John's *Spritual Canticle* stands along with Augustine's *Confessions*, the writings of Hildegard of Bingen and Julian of Norwich, and the *Cloud of Unknowing* as some of the greatest spiritual writing in the Western mystical tradition. John became infected by Teresa's yearnings for reform and worked diligently within the male Carmelite order while Teresa reformed the convent. As is indicated by this quote from *The Interior Castle*, Teresa never lost sight of the greatness of our humanity united with that of Christ:

> As he himself says, he created us in his image and likeness. Now if this is so, and it is, there is no point in our fatiguing ourselves by attempting to comprehend the beauty of this castle; for though it is his creature, and there is therefore as much difference between it and God as between creature and Creator, the very fact that His Majesty says it is made in his image means that we can hardly form any conception of the soul's great dignity and beauty.

Teresa's words stand in sharp contrast to the dark imaginings of John Calvin.

Another Spaniard in the forefront of reform, Ignatius of Loyola found himself with a lot of time on his hands as he was in convalescence from an injury received in battle. Being a man of action and a Roman Catholic of his times, Ignatius had no real familiarity with the Scriptures until he found a life of Christ and a book about saints that would be his only reading materials to help him pass his days while recuperating. As so often happens through an encounter with the living word, Ignatius's life was transformed. His desire for an ever deeper relationship with Jesus led to the creation of the Jesuits—a new religious order of men who pledged themselves to serve the pope as his personal "army" to combat the heresies unleashed by the Protestant reformers.

Men joining the order were subject to a rigorous ten-year period of formation. Before becoming a full-fledged member, the postulant candidate had a thorough initiation into the Catholic Christian faith through both the head and the heart. As the Jesuit order evolved, the freedom from the accountability to particular bishops, coupled with the reputation Jesuits earned for a sound command of Christian doctrine made them ideal candidates for missionary work in the lands now being opened to European exploration, colonization, and commerce.

Jesuit priests such as Francis Xavier and Matteo Ricci in the Far East and Isaac Jogues in the New World were able to adapt the basic tenets of the Christian faith to a wide variety of cultures that was very different from Christianity's Western Europe. In so doing, these missionaries were at the forefront of the efforts to take Jesus' command to proclaim the gospel "to all nations" to a new level, and thus lay the groundwork for the truly global Church of the twenty-first century. (In today's world, seventy percent or more of all Catholics live somewhere other than in Western Europe.) The Jesuit efforts at separating the essence of the faith from its cultural packaging threatened the Spanish colonial rulers and bishops of Central and South America who felt that acculturating the subjugated native population was essential to controlling them. It is a great irony that the same Spanish Church that nurtured the Jesuits in the order's infancy successfully pressured the pope into suppressing the order for a while in the late 1700s.

Trent 1545

Building a Better Mousetrap

By the time the Council of Trent was convened in 1545, to provide an official, coordinated response to almost thirty years of Protestant development, any hope or desire for reconciliation within the hierarchy of the Roman Catholic Church had long since evaporated. Nevertheless some genuine reform of the immediate causes of the Reformation did take place during the three sessions of the council held intermittently between 1545 and 1563. By promulgating the first comprehensive catechisms, which among other things defined the seven sacraments, most particularly the Church's understanding of the Eucharist, the council did provide the faithful with a much needed roadmap through the complicated forest of Church doctrine.

Trent took definite steps to avoid a muddying of the waters in the future by requiring that every diocese establish a seminary for the formation and training of priests and by requiring bishops to live in the dioceses they were responsible for shepherding. Celibacy was enforced with renewed vigor. The worldliness of the papacy was transformed by a series of reform-minded popes such as the Dutch Adrian I (the last non-Italian pope before John Paul II) and Paul III whose personal lives were characterized much more by asceticism than hedonism.

In the end, however, what the Council of Trent succeeded in doing was to build a better mousetrap. Church doctrine and the teachings of the pope and bishops would be more comprehensible and consistent with the basic tenets of the Christian faith, and room for abuse would be lessened. No real attempt was made, however, to articulate a new vision of what it meant to be Church. It would be another four hundred years before the people of God would fully come to terms with the death of the medieval model of Church and begin to reflect upon the crucial question in earnest: "What does it mean to be the body of Christ in the modern world?" A Herculean, Spirit-led effort on the parts of both laity and clergy would be necessary in order to begin to create a new mindset in the Church capable of addressing this question.

For Thought and Discussion

1) Do you know of any women in today's Church and world who speak truth to power as Catherine of Siena did? In your opinion, what do such women need to say?

2) In both the Avignon papacy and the Great Western Schism the role of the pope changed. What is the pope's role today and what do you base this on?

3) Reflect on John 3:16 (For God so loved the world...). What does it mean to you? In what ways is the Church today proclaiming this message?

4) Are there elements of vending-machine Christianity in the Church today? in your spiritual life? What are they?

5) What images of God—biblical or otherwise—have great meaning for you? Why?

6) Discuss the role of the magisterium and the faithful in forming the *sensus fidei* of this period.

Part Three

The Modern Church

SEVEN

"Holy" War?

Christians living in the shadow of 9/11, and caught up in the tragedies which are the product of the war on terrorism, sometimes shake their heads in wonder. How could a religion based on the fundamental righteousness and benevolence of God be used as a license to kill those who hold contrasting beliefs? When such thoughts tempt us toward a spirit of self-righteousness, it's important to remember that the same bloody impulse casts a long shadow in the history of the Christian Church as well.

The tumult of the Protestant Reformation reached a form of a cease-fire in 1555 when under the terms of the Peace of Augsburg, every German prince was permitted to adopt either Lutheranism or Roman Catholicism as the official religion of his province. This uneasy truce created a kind of Catholic-Protestant checkerboard across the realm of the Holy Roman Empire, but the compromise was destined to be short-lived. Pressure from the staunchly Roman Catholic Spanish part of the empire and the burgeoning Protestant Churches adopting Calvin's model—sometimes in direct conflict with Lutheran Churches—made violence between neighboring provinces almost inevitable. The mounting tensions resulted in the formation of the Protestant Union in 1608 and, in response, the creation of the Catholic League among the Roman Catholic princes of northern Europe.

Among the tatters of what once had been Christendom, the legacy of intertwining powers of Church and state assured the mixing of religious motives with political motives. Roman Catholic and Protestant princes trying to assure the continued independence of their home turf came into armed conflict beginning in 1618. By the time the Peace of Westphalia was signed in 1648, the devastation relative to the overall population of Western Europe is estimated by historians to be on a par with that of World War II. (The population of what is today the nations of Germany and Austria, for example, was slashed by about a third. This percentage translates into millions of deaths.)

The Peace of Westphalia is a turning point in a number of respects. The political reorganization promoted by the treaty resulted in the collapse of the Holy Roman Empire and the emergence of the modern European states. The horrific display of barbarism among supposedly Christian nations bred a deep and abiding cynicism among many in Europe toward organized Christianity in general, and this would result in the almost wholesale rejection of the Church by the great thinkers of the Enlightenment.

Most important of all for our story, however, the Peace signified the beginnings of a new model within the Church. Enshrined in the general support of religious tolerance within the accord was a hard-won recognition that "holy war"—that is, violence in the name of God—never was and could never be an authentic response of Christian discipleship or an effective means of evangelization. Although such a recognition has not prevented Christian nations from continuing to go to war, it has prevented them from dragging God *explicitly* into the conflict. In the centuries since the accord was signed, the Church has returned to its roots and placed itself firmly on the side of peaceful resolution of conflict.

In the Beginning

> You have heard that it was said, "You shall love your neighbor and hate your enemy." But I say to you, Love your enemies and pray for those who persecute you, so that you may be children of your Father in heaven; for he makes his sun rise on the evil and on the good, and sends rain on the righteous and on the unrighteous. For if you love those who love you, what reward do you have? Do not even the tax-collectors do

the same? And if you greet only your brothers and sisters, what more are you doing than others? Do not even the Gentiles do the same? Be perfect, therefore, as your heavenly Father is perfect. (Matthew 5:43–48)

How a movement that bases its moral code on these words of Jesus could become the force behind one of the bloodiest wars in the history of Western Europe requires some critical analysis of Christian history. During the first two centuries of the Church's existence Christians were often pacifists, enjoying the same exemption that Jews did from serving in the auxiliary forces assisting the Roman army. (Recall that Christianity was viewed by the Romans as a sect of Judaism for about almost two hundred years after its inception.) This commitment to pacifism remains to this day a vibrant and growing strain within the Church and is the particular charism of the Christian sect commonly referred to as the Quakers. During the time of the persecutions, the Christian martyrs were venerated for their refusal to use violence even in an effort to defend their own lives.

With the establishment of Christianity as the official religion of the Roman Empire, however, this position proved to be increasingly untenable. More and more of the officials who ran the Roman government, including its military leaders, became Christians. Frontiers needed to be defended as the empire faced almost incessant threats from either the Germanic tribes to the north or the Parthians and later Sassanids to the East. Piracy in the Mediterranean was kept under control only by the strict vigilance of the Roman navy.

As exemplified by the troubles of Pope Leo the Great, after the Western Roman Empire collapsed, the Church had the responsibility of meeting not only the spiritual needs of the empire but its physical needs as well, including security. In 753, Pope Stephen II accepted the Donation of Pepin in an effort to more permanently meet these needs amid the chaos that followed Rome's collapse. The Church now possessed its own worldly kingdom—the Papal States—and a standing army to defend it. Increasingly, therefore, as the era of the Roman Empire gave way to the early medieval period, the Church was forced to grapple with an uncomfortable question: Under what conditions is it morally permissible for a Christian to take up arms?

Just War Theory

Beginning with the thoughts of Augustine in the fourth century and expanded upon most notably by Thomas Aquinas in the thirteenth century, the Church developed what would become known as the "just war theory." The basic idea behind the theory is a long-standing Judeo-Christian interpretation of the fifth commandment as meaning "Thou shalt not *murder*." God never permits the taking of an innocent life. Should force be necessary to disable or even kill an aggressor who would otherwise do harm to the believer or to the community, however, physical force could be justified.

Just as an *individual* might unfortunately find it necessary at times to use force to stop an aggressor, so might a *community* beset by an aggressive tribe, nation, or authority wishing to do it harm. The tenets of the just war theory apply very specific and demanding criteria that must be satisfied in order for a Christian community to take up arms. While the particulars of the theory have been expressed in different ways at different times in Church history, the essential principles go something like this:

- *War is always a last resort.* The Christian presumption must always be *against going to war.* If there is any way to eliminate the threat through negotiation or diplomacy or some sort of punitive but nonviolent sanctions, then these methods must be exhausted before war can be declared.

- *War can only be declared for a just cause.* War must only be declared for *defensive* reasons (to protect innocent lives or to preserve conditions necessary for a decent standard of living) and never for *offensive* reasons (to gain territory or wealth).

- *War can only be declared by a legitimate authority.* Individual citizens or subjects can never take up arms as a mob but must be obeying the declarations of those entrusted with responsibility for governing.

- *There must be a reasonable possibility of success.* Given the terrible toll on life and property that war inevitably takes, there is no morally justifiable reason to enter into a war the Christian state or kingdom cannot win. To do so would simply be a decision to send innocent people to be slaughtered.

The above principles govern the decision to go to war. Once that decision is made, there are several other principles that govern the manner in which Christians must fight a war:

- *The response must be proportional to the threat.* As would be true in a case of personal self-defense, only the force required to stop the aggressor is morally permissible. Any further use of physical force, no matter how heinous we might perceive the aggressor to be, takes us from *justice* to *vengeance.*

- *War must be conducted with a right intention.* Closely related to the above principle and echoing the belief behind the ninth and tenth commandments is the requirement that military action is never influenced by a desire to seek revenge against an enemy, but always by a desire to promote the common good. Attitudes and actions are always closely connected.

- *Civilians always have immunity in any war.* Battles must be limited to engagements with the soldiers of the opposing army. Civilians can never be targeted or intentionally placed in harm's way.

Any brief overview of Western European history will demonstrate that these criteria were observed more by exception than by rule. Too often local feudal lords and later the kings of the emerging nations of modern Europe entered into any number of armed conflicts—sometimes directly aided by papal troops for reasons that had more to do with personal gain or national interest than the common good. Yet throughout this bloody history of warfare, the ideals of the just war theory endured. We see them captured in the legends surrounding King Arthur and his knights of the roundtable in Camelot. The code of chivalry that developed during the medieval period is another articulation of these principles. We can hear echoes of this in the various rules of engagement hammered out in the Geneva conventions of the last century.

External Crusades

The development of the just war theory was an attempt to forge a basic compromise between Christian values and the reality of warfare in Western Europe. Beginning in the eleventh century, the idea of a just war took on a new dimension when in 1095 Pope Urban II announced his intention to raise an army of Crusaders who would liberate Jerusalem from the control of the Muslim "infidels" who ruled it. As an extra incentive, the pope announced that a special indulgence would be granted that would result in the complete remission of punishment for sins due in purgatory for any soldier who participated in this Crusade. (Remember that the Crusades took place during the time when vending-machine Christianity was at its height.) The period of the Crusades lasted well into the fourteenth century.

Essentially, the idea of a Crusade, or "holy" war, expanded the idea of an unjust aggressor in a dangerous way. No longer did the term only apply to an impending threat to the temporal security of Europe; the Muslims had long since ceased their attempts to conquer Christian lands. This time, the threat was to the *spiritual* security of the faithful. If Christian pilgrims could no longer go on pilgrimage to the birthplace of Jesus and of the Church—the Muslim ban on pilgrimages was an immediate cause of the first Crusade—they could no longer gain the indulgences attached to those pilgrimages. From the point of view of medieval Christianity, their spiritual welfare was thus in jeopardy. (It's worth noting that for hundreds of years prior to this change in Muslim policy the "infidels" did allow Christians safe passage into the Holy Land.)

Expanding the just war theory to include so-called holy wars was a horrific development. Now a just war no longer had to be based on an objective physical threat. Christians could take up arms in the face of a perceived *spiritual* threat, if exhorted to do so by the pope. From the eleventh century right up until the Peace of Westphalia this expansion of the just war theory legitimized a steady stream of bloodshed, first between Christians and Muslims, then within the Roman Catholic Church itself, and finally between Roman Catholics and Protestants.

Although the first Crusade did achieve its goal of conquering Jerusalem and the surrounding lands, the victory came at a great price. Many of the Crusaders never made it to Jerusalem but died from heatstroke or dehydration or disease on the way. When Jerusalem fell, the Crusaders conducted an indiscriminate slaughter of the city's Muslim inhabitants. The Crusaders also unleashed their fury on the small Jewish community in Jerusalem, justified in their own minds by a millennium of Christian anti-Semitism aimed at the "Christ-killers."

Later Crusades were also bloody, but did not have much success in achieving their military objectives. The entire enterprise reached its nadir in the abomination of the fourth Crusade. During this campaign of the early thirteenth century, the Crusaders never made it to the Holy Land, but did manage to utterly destroy Constantinople, the great *Christian* city with a history dating back to the time of Constantine himself. As discussed in Chapter Four, relations between Eastern Orthodox and Roman Catholic Christians never recovered from this blow.

Internal Crusades

If Crusades could be justified against external spiritual threats, they could also be justified against spiritual threats to the orthodox faith within the Roman Catholic Church. Beginning in the thirteenth century, movements deemed heretical by the magisterium of the Church began to proliferate. Many were motivated by a revulsion toward the vending-machine Roman Catholicism of the period, some by political considerations, others by a "millenarianism" spirit that anticipated the imminent arrival of the kingdom of God. By far the most intractable heretical movement was that of the Cathari ("pure ones") centered around the city of Albi in southern France.

The theology of the Cathari was really a renewal of the Gnosticism that had plagued the Church in its infancy. As discussed in Chapter Three, gnosticism holds that a sharp distinction existed between the material world, which was inherently evil, and the spiritual realm, which was inherently good. Besides the enduring nature of this philosophy, the particular popularity of the Cathari was their call for reform of a Church which was becoming more and more preoccupied with worldly affairs and seemingly less and less with its fundamentally spiritual mission. The Church was threatened by the Cathari on two levels. Theologically, gnosticism cannot accommodate any belief in the Incarnation because such a sacred union of flesh and spirit is an impossibility. Practically, the Cathari insistence on a radical reform of the Church hierarchy was a direct threat to papal power and influence.

In large part the emphasis on education that became the hallmark of the mendicant religious order founded by Dominic de Guzman was inspired by these troubling developments in Albi. Dominic was convinced that the only way to defeat the Cathari was to proclaim the Christian gospel with greater clarity so that the faithful could focus more deeply on the mystery of the Incarnation. The Dominicans and many like-minded Christians committed themselves to the only formula that has ever succeeded in converting minds and hearts: proclaim the gospel, live the gospel, and trust in Jesus' promise that, "I am with you always."

Unfortunately the spirit of the Age of Crusades was not influenced sufficiently by the Spirit. Led by Simon de Montfort and King Louis VIII of France, the Albigensian Crusades began in 1209 and lasted until 1229. The Crusaders, with the blessing of the papacy, hunted down the Cathari with a ruthless determination to either convert them at the point of the sword or to exterminate them. Much blood was shed before the Crusade was halted by Pope Innocent III.

The Inquisition

How doth the Church presume to examine by this foreign judgment the hearts of men? Or how is it that the Cathari are given no legitimate respite for deliberation but are burned immediately?

These words by a contemporary witness to the slaughter of the Albigensian Crusades, Peter Cantor (as quoted in *A History of Christianity*), concisely capture the reason why "holy" war of any kind can never be reconciled with authentic Christian discipleship. How can one look inside another human heart? All that the Church can ever do, and at times must do, is to make judgments on the words and actions of the believer in relation to the gospel message.

Time and time again the Scriptures portray a savior who looks at the heart and thus sees not through human eyes but through the eyes of God. As has been illustrated in this book numerous times (think of the apostate crisis or the founding of the mendicant orders), it often takes time—generations, in some cases—for the *sensus fidei* to catch up with the movement of the Spirit.

In bringing the Albigensian Crusades to an end in 1229, Pope Innocent III recognized half of the wisdom in Peter Cantor's reflections. To indiscriminately slaughter without benefit of trial meant that the process of weeding out heresy was left to the whims or illicit motivations of the mob. (Some of the women killed during the Albigensian Crusade as heretics, for example, were turned in by priests whose sexual advances had been spurned.) Innocent authorized the creation of the Inquisition, an office within the hierarchy of the Church empowered to conduct in-depth and unbiased investigations of charges of heresy and to exonerate, imprison, or execute the accused as the evidence required.

Although eventually the Inquisition would become notorious for its abuses, harsh methods of torture, and brutal executions of innocent women and men, the system of justice established by the Church compares favorably to the rudimentary or non-existent judicial systems of the Middle Ages. At least the process offered some opportunity for rational and impartial investigation, something the average European could not count on from local authorities.

A Legacy of Terror

The reforms by Pope Innocent III, however, had done nothing to deal with the more intractable problem associated with the Crusades. Only God can judge the human heart. Furthermore, conversion to the gospel is either a choice freely made by an individual in response to the love of Christ or it is not genuine. Even if every charge of heresy brought before the tribunals of the Inquisition were motivated by a loving concern for the common good (but often weren't), there is no way that Christianity can be forged at the point of a sword or by the threat of being burned at the stake.

The most celebrated miscarriage of justice during this period is the martyrdom of Joan of Arc. At the time that she was pronounced a heretic and burned at the stake, the official charge centered on her claim to have heard the voices of angels and saints, particularly that of Michael the Archangel, who had directed her to lead the charge at the battle of Orleans. It is clear now, hundreds of years later, that the young "maid of Orleans" was caught up in the political machinations of the French and English powers of the time. Furthermore, her claim of personal revelation could never have been reconciled with the understanding of the faith held by popes and bishops who saw themselves as the "pipes" through which God bestowed grace upon the faithful.

Here again is the error pointed out by Peter Cantor in reflecting on the Albigensian Crusades. It is one thing for the magisterium of the Church to declare that private revelations are not reconcilable with essential Christian doctrine; it is something very different to declare that such revelation cannot occur. Such a declaration arrogantly presumes to know the mind of Christ and the movement of the Holy Spirit within the human heart.

In addition to Joan—declared the patron saint of France in the twentieth century—there were many lesser-known victims of the Inquisition. In Spain, under the auspices of the Dominican friar Torquemada, the Inquisition became a means by which the Church could eliminate Protestant reformers. (Ironically, many Dominicans were appointed by the papacy as Inquisitors because of their reputation for a thorough understanding of Christian doctrine!) In the event of plague or unusual natural phenomena, the Inquisition became the instrument through which the local church could calm the fears of the populace by rounding up a few suspected witches and burning them at the stake.

The influence of the Inquisition eventually faded. The emphasis on reason inspired by advances in science during the Renaissance and the Age of Enlightenment discredited the whole idea that it was possible to prove or disprove divine revelation. Even the concept of divine revelation itself came under intense scrutiny. It was not until the nineteenth century, however, that the last cases were brought before the Inquisition in Spain.

The Light at the End of the Tunnel

The repudiation of holy war enshrined in the Peace of Westphalia received another boost when the Church ceased to be a temporal kingdom in 1878. (More about this in Chapter Eight.) As the Church has lost most of its responsibilities as a state, we have become free to once again be the leaven in the world Christ calls us to be. The last two centuries, and especially the twentieth century, have seen a fundamental shift in the role the Church has played in response to warfare in the modern world. A magnificent *sensus fidei* has been developing within the Church that repudiates war in all of its forms.

A major turning point was reached during the pontificate of Pope Benedict XV, whose papacy spanned the tragic events of World War I and its aftermath. Benedict tirelessly worked for peace during the conflict, using all of the influence he could muster as a mediator behind the scenes. When peace was finally achieved, he courageously and prophetically spoke out against the terribly punitive terms of the Treaty of Versailles. Anthony Gilles points out the magnitude of the change evident in Benedict's words and actions: "Benedict was wise enough to understand that God was on the side of neither set of combatants. For the first time in centuries, a pope refused to involve the papacy—whether militarily, politically or rhetorically—in a major European war" (*The People of Hope*, p. 77).

Benedict's commitment to peace was reaffirmed in Pope John XXIII's encyclical *Pacem in Terris* and in the strong support for international mediation as a means to handle conflicts between nations proclaimed in the *Pastoral Constitution on the Church in the Modern World* (*Guadium et spes*) promulgated at Vatican Council II. During his long pontificate, John Paul II on many occasions amplified the Church's exhortation to seek peaceful means to resolve the world's conflicts, perhaps never more passionately then in the words he wrote in his encyclical *Centesimus Annus* in 1991:

> I myself, on the occasion of the recent tragic war in the Persian Gulf, repeated the cry: "War—never again!" No, never again war, which destroys the lives of innocent people, teaches how to kill, throws into upheaval even the lives of those who do the killing and leaves behind a trail of resentment and hatred, thus making it all the more difficult to find a just solution of the very problems which provoked the war." (Sec. 52)

As we continue to reflect on the gospels and on the exhortations of the magisterium, there grows a greater and greater desire among the faithful to be peacemakers and to critically examine the stated justifications of governments that declare war. Groups such as Pax Christi provide a vehicle through which these anti-war sentiments can be introduced into the public forum in a spirit of Christian charity.

The Middle Ages saw the rise of the just war theory. Today more and more Christians and other women and men of good will are growing in the conviction that a "just war" is an oxymoron. This change of mind—happening both within the magisterium and the *sensus fidelium*—offers great hope for a future that more truly incarnates the "peace" that the risen Christ announced to his first disciples.

For Thought and Discussion

1) Describe several ways in which the Peace of Westphalia was a turning point for the Church and the world.

2) Do some research on pacifism in the Church. In particular focus on
   - Quaker spirituality
   - Pax Christi
   - U.S. bishop's peace pastoral "The Challenge of Peace" (available at www.usccb.org)

3) Review the basic principles of the just war theory. Given the realities of modern warfare, has the just war theory become obsolete? Explain why or why not.

4) What is your reaction to this statement: "Force is sometimes necessary in maintaining the integrity of the Catholic Church." Give reasons supporting and opposing the statement.

5) Were you aware of the reasons for the Crusades? Compare these to the "war on terrorism." Are there similarities? differences?

6) Where in the Church today do you think the Spirit is calling us to develop a new *sensus fidei*? Which partner—the magisterium or the faithful—seems to be taking the lead in the journey toward a fuller understanding of the workings of the Spirit? Why do you think this?

EIGHT

Beyond Vatican II

The Church took its lumps in the eighteenth and nineteenth centuries. The concepts of divine revelation and absolute authority granted by God to any particular ruling class were assailed from a number of directions. Politically, this was the age of revolution, as one emerging nation state after another began to throw off the yoke of monarchs claiming to rule by divine decree and replacing them with more democratic forms of government. The very idea of "absolute truth," at least as far as governance was concerned, was replaced by the belief that the most effective means of creating a just society is the consensus of a citizenry enlightened by reason and a concern for the common good. The clearest and most profound expression of this new mindset is found in the Declaration of Independence and later the Constitution of the newly-founded republic of the United States of America.

Scientifically, the Age of Enlightenment built on the work of such pioneers as Galileo and Sir Isaac Newton whose meticulous observations and measurements of natural pheonomena struck a serious blow to the belief that the Bible was the fount of all Truth. In the sixteenth century, Galileo used his newly designed telescopes to empirically prove the theory of Nicolas Copernicus that the universe was in fact heliocentric (the earth revolves around the sun) and not geocentric (the sun and planets revolve around the earth). About a century later, Sir Isaac

111

Newton laid out the basic principles of physics, which demonstrated that a wide variety of natural phenomena could be measured and predicted according to mathematical formulas and careful observation, and were not directly dependent on some mysterious will of God.

If the Bible could be demonstrated to be in error in its interpretations of the natural world, many began to wonder if its insights into spiritual truths were suspect as well.

The work of Galileo, Newton, and their contemporaries was only the first wave of critical skepticism directed toward the Bible, however. By the beginning of the nineteenth century, scientists in the newly founded disciplines of geology and paleontology had conclusively proven that the earth was much older than the thousands of years suggested by the Bible—millions of years older, in fact. Then in the middle of the nineteenth century Charles Darwin introduced his theory of evolution in *The Origin of Species* based on his nature studies in the Galapagos Islands. The implications of Darwin's work, still being felt to this day, were startling. If human beings have evolved from more primitive forms of life, then the Bible's conception of humanity's "fall from grace" may actually have the story backwards. In evolutionary terms, the very recent development of consciousness suggests that we do not yet know what being "fully human" means!

All of these developments, of course, followed on the heels of the Protestant Reformation and the bloody battles among Christians that left large number of Western Europeans questioning the legitimacy of organized religion in general. How could a faith founded on a belief in God's unconditional love and in universal sister and brotherhood have been the catalyst for so much bloodshed?

On the Defensive

Into this maelstrom came Giovanni Maria Mastia-Ferretti, who took the name Pius IX upon his election to the papacy in 1846. During his long pontificate, which lasted until 1878, Pius IX set the tone for an era in which the magisterium of the Church remained almost perpetually on the defensive. The modern world was the enemy, in particular the philosophy of Liberalism and, in a later incarnation, Modernism. Defining either term precisely is difficult, but both involved an embrace of modern political, scientific, and cultural ideas that posed a threat to established ways of thinking about divinely ordained authority and revelation within the Church. Gregory XVI, a predecessor of Pius IX, referred to Liberalism as, "This false and absurd maxim, or better this madness, that everyone should have and practice freedom of conscience."

Pius's anger and genuine concern for the faithful coalesced in an encyclical entitled *Quanta Cura* released on December 8, 1864. (On December 8, 1854, he had proclaimed as infallible the Roman Catholic belief in the Immaculate Conception of Mary.) At the conclusion of the encyclical, the pope attached a *Syllabus of Errors* which condemned in more specific language eighty particular ideas, including the following:

- The Church should be separated from the State and the State from the Church. (#55)

- In this our age it is no longer expedient that the Catholic religion should be treated as the only religion of the State. (#77)

- The Roman pontiff can and ought to recognize and harmonize himself with progress, with liberalism, and with modern civilization. (#80) (quoted in *People of Hope* by Anthony E. Gilles, p. 46)

Clearly the hierarchy of the Roman Catholic Church saw no common ground between the major movements and currents of the modern world and the Church itself. In fact, there were real dangers to the Christian faith contained within the broad philosophy of Liberalism. Remember that this was the age of Karl Marx who wrote in his *Communist Manifesto* that religion was a fraud, the "opiate of the people," designed to keep the wealthy in power and the poor content with their lot. Friedrich Nietzsche and his disciples were laying down the principles of modern atheism. The abuses of the Reign of Terror during the French Revolution in which thousands of people lost their lives to the guillotine, horrifically demonstrated that eliminating organized religion in no way guaranteed that reason would triumph over a mob mentality.

Yet a number of the pope's contemporaries saw his absolute rejection of Liberalism as too extreme. Some theologians and more progressive bishops interested in bridging the gap between modern society as a whole and the Church downplayed the document or ignored it altogether. Cardinal John Henry Newman, the famous English convert who had his own doubts about Liberalism, offered this caution in one of his writings:

Many a man has ideas, which he hopes are true, and useful for his day....He is willing, or rather would be thankful, to give them up, if they can be proved to be erroneous or dangerous, and by means of controversy he obtains his end. He is answered and he yields or on the contrary he finds that he is considered safe. He would not dare to do this if he knew an authority, which was supreme and final, was watching every word he said, and made signs of assent or dissent to each sentence, as he uttered it. (quoted in *Papal Sin* by Garry Wills, p. 268)

The best way to confront the excesses of Liberalism, in other words, is to create a climate of mutual trust in which ideas can be articulated and examined in the light of both faith and reason.

Pope Pius IX, however, was in no mood to compromise. He convened the First Vatican Council on December 8, 1869, in order to define Catholic doctrine more clearly, with particular emphasis on how it contradicted the spirit of the modern world. In 1870, the council promulgated a constitution entitled *Dei Filius*, a document that denounced Liberalism while updating developments in Catholic doctrine since the Council of Trent. Next the council produced *Pastor Aeternus*, the document that defined papal infallibility. Sensing that the pope had pushed the definition too far, one fifth of the bishops in attendance circulated a petition asking that it be eliminated. When that failed, sixty bishops left Rome secretly so as not to be required to vote!

The council's proceedings came to a grinding halt on September 20, 1870, when troops involved in the Italian Unification movement (who had conquered the Papal States in order to incorporate them into the unified nation of Italy) were reported to be fast approaching Rome. With the collapse of the council's proceedings, any hope of modifying the pope's anti-modern stance was gone for the rest of his pontificate.

New Things

In 1891, Pius's successor Leo XIII issued an encyclical entitled *Rerum Novarum*. While Leo was no more comfortable with Liberalism than Pius IX was, he was pragmatic enough to recognize that the magisterium's determination to keep the Church untainted by the modern world had an unfortunate side effect. In the increasingly pluralistic and democratic marketplace of ideas, the Spirit-filled voice of the Church was becoming more and more marginalized. The primary purpose of Leo's letter was to offer insight into the effects of the burgeoning Industrial Revolution on the human person from the perspective of the gospel and Church tradition. The encyclical's title (in English, "New Things") would also apply well, however, to the new approach Pope Leo XIII adopted in advancing the teaching of the Church.

Today, *Rerum Novarum* is considered the first "social encyclical." These letters, including but not limited to *Pacem et Terris* by John XXIII, *Populorum Progressio* by Paul VI, and *Centesimus Annus* by John Paul II articulate and apply basic Christian moral principles governing social justice to the particular issues and controversies of the day. Rather than issuing wholesale condemnations of the modern world, these encyclicals invite dialogue, repositioning the magisterium as a teacher in the best sense of the term. They exhort the faithful, and through their efforts, the world at large, to consider fundamental political, economic, and social developments from the standpoint of how these policies affect the dignity of the human person, in particular the poorest of the poor. Rather than provide infallible pronouncements and judgments, the social encyclicals repeatedly proclaim in the form of several basic principles the Christian understanding of the sacredness of the human person and his or her intimate relationship with God and with one another. They include:

Personalism: an individual's right to exist as a free and autonomous person must always be paramount.

Subsidiarity: no higher or more complex form of social organization can usurp the function of a lower, less complex organization.

Solidarity: all are united to mutually binding responsibilities to safeguard the worth of each person. We are our sister's and brother's keeper.

Common Good: Pope John XXIII defined this as the "aggregate of those social presuppositions which make possible or easier for people to achieve the full development of their values." Christians have an obligation to earnestly seek, promote, and protect the common good.

Universal Solidarity: no particular society has the right to deny the citizens of any other society the same degree of personal integrity it grants its own members. This principle is becoming increasingly relevant and pressing in a world where the developed countries of the West consume the resources of the earth at a far greater rate than their percentage of the earth's population would justify.

Throughout the twentieth century, the magisterium has developed a number of more particular principles from these far-ranging ideas.

The second innovation in Leo's encyclical was the pope's bestowal of the Church's blessing on the various Catholic action movements that were forming among the laity. These movements, particularly those aiming to improve the conditions of the worker in a time before labor unions and collective bargaining agreements, were based on the belief that just as members of the clergy and religious life have unique and holy callings from God, so too do the laity. Given their political, economic, and social interactions with the world, the laity, in carrying out their own apostolate, are in a uniquely effective position to be the "leaven" that would bring Christ to the world and thus transform it.

This emerging understanding of the lay apostolate is in sharp contrast to the vending-machine mentality that had influenced both the hierarchy of the Church and the people for so many centuries. If the pope and bishops are the only "pipes" through which God's grace flows, there is no reason to engage the laity in any meaningful formation or catechesis. "Formation" under such a mindset consists in teaching the laity how to "turn on the faucet" through the rote memorization of certain doctrines and mechanical instruction on how to receive the sacraments and attend liturgy.

Learning to Dance 1965

Vatican Council II marked a maturation of a *sensus fidei* within the Church that recognized the "call to holiness" of all Christian women and men. The council described the vocation of the laity this way:

> Christ, the great prophet, who proclaimed the kingdom of his Father both by the testimony of his life and the power of his words, continually fulfills his prophetic office until the complete manifestation of glory. He does this not only through the hierarchy who teach in his name and with his authority, but also through the laity whom he made his witnesses and to whom he gave understanding of the faith (*sensus fidei*) and an

attractiveness in speech (c. Acts 2:17–18; Revelation 19:10), so that the power of the Gospel might shine forth in their daily social and family life. (*Lumen gentium*, Sect. 35)

Rather than affirm the Church as a pyramid through which grace and holiness flow from the top down, the council called for Catholics to recapture the spirit of the early centuries of Christianity during which those in ordained ministry and those called to live out their vocations in the world stood side by side in a more collegial solidarity. The vocations of clergy and laity are different, but each partner in the dance of faith hears the same voice of the Spirit in his or her heart, and each has something important to say to the other. Just as Jesus unites humanity and God in his person, so the Spirit invites the ordained and the laity together to incarnate the body of Christ in the world.

This fundamental changing of our mind as a Church has borne great fruit. Consider for example the life of Dorothy Day. With the help of her mentor Peter Maurin and the dedicated efforts of a host of mostly lay volunteers, she established a number of houses of hospitality to provide food, clothing, shelter, and meaningful labor to some of the millions of unemployed and destitute caught in the throes of the Great Depression. She founded the *Catholic Worker* newspaper aimed at disseminating the social justice teachings of the Church to the faithful and to the world at large. Later in her life she became active in the nuclear non-proliferation and civil rights movements, even spending nights in a jail cell for her actions.

Dorothy Day's life also gives witness to the path Christian discipleship might take in a time of transition. Searching for meaning but uncertain where to find it, Dorothy devoted herself to the causes of social justice. She worked on behalf of the same abused workers Pope Leo XIII hoped to defend through her brief affiliation with the Communist party in America and also through her efforts as a suffragette during the campaign to bring women the vote in the second and third decades of the twentieth century. It was not until her life had been shattered by an abortion and, some years later, by her heart-wrenching decision to leave her common-law husband and father of her daughter, Tamar, that she embraced the Catholic faith and was baptized. (You can read the story of Dorothy's life in her autobiography, *The Long Loneliness*.)

Learning to Fly

As was also true in the early Church, the laity today have taken their places alongside priests and religious as martyrs for the faith. Perhaps the best-known of these are the El Salvador martyrs from the 1970s and 1980s. The terrible economic injustice in El Salvador was that ninety percent of the land was in the hands of about twelve powerful families. This reduced millions of El Salvadorans to lives of hopeless poverty. As both Pope Paul VI and Pope John Paul II have repeatedly pointed out, just as peace is the inevitable result of justice, war is the inevitable result of injustice. When civil war finally did break out in El Salvador in the late1970s, it was greatly exacerbated by the politics of the "Cold War" between the United States and Russia. American arms flooded into the country to prop up a government that was democratic in name but that had never allowed a free and fair election. Soviet arms were equally available to the Marxist guerillas intent on redistributing wealth at the point of a gun.

The overwhelming majority of El Salvadorans were Roman Catholic, giving the Church an opportunity and a responsibility to be the voice of the poor and a champion for peace and justice. Leading the effort was Archbishop Oscar Romero, a shy and studious man who only slowly came to understand the injustice. Once he accepted this, he galvanized the effort to transform El Salvador. His fervent and dedicated opposition to the killing and injustice ultimately cost him his life when, on March 24, 1980, he was assassinated while presiding at a celebration of the Eucharist. Within the same year, four women working for justice and peace in El Salvador (Maryknoll Sisters Ita Ford and Maura Clarke, Ursuline Sister Dorothy Kazel, and lay missionary Jean Donovan) were brutally raped and murdered as well. United in life by the call to bring Christ's peace and healing to a terribly wounded land, and united in death among the communion of saints, these five Christian disciples— ordained, religious, and lay—provide us with an inspiring example of the call to holiness shared by all members of the body of Christ.

The Light of the Nations

Vatican Council II, convened by Pope John XXIII in 1962 and concluded by Pope Paul VI in 1965, took a battle ax to the remnants of vending-machine Christianity. Responding to a Spirit-inspired perception of the signs of the times, Pope John XXIII called the faithful to a thorough *aggiornamento*. This "updating" of our understanding of what it means to be the body of Christ was to be accomplished through both an in-depth examination of the Church, *ad intra* (within itself) and *ad extra* (in relation to the world). Each of the four primary documents of the council looked back to the time before the Edict of Milan but also looked ahead to where the Spirit seemed to be leading.

Sacrosanctum concilium (Constitution on the Sacred Liturgy) brought to fruition the reform movement aimed at bringing the laity back to full participation in the celebration of the Eucharist, the "source and summit" of all Christian life. This movement had received a great impetus from the decrees issued by Pope Pius X in the early part of the twentieth century. *Dei verbum* (Dogmatic Constitution on Divine Revelation) attempted to bridge the gap between the Scriptures and the faithful by presenting the fruits of over a century of prayerful and intelligent Bible scholarship within the Church and by exhorting Catholics to regularly read and prayerfully reflect on the Word of God. From the very opening line of *Guadium et spes* (Pastoral Constitution on the Church in the Modern World), the council rejected the mindset rooted in the Protestant Reformation that saw the Church and the modern world as diametrically opposed: "The joys and the hopes, the griefs and the anxieties of the men [and women] of this age, especially those who are poor or in any way afflicted, these too are the joys and hopes, the griefs and anxieties of the followers of Christ. Indeed, nothing genuinely human fails to raise an echo in their hearts" (#1).

At last, there is the evidence of a profound change in the way Roman Catholics understand the nature of Church found in the fourth primary document, *Lumen gentium* (Dogmatic Constitution on the Church). Setting the tone with four biblical images of the Church as a "sheepfold whose one and indispensable door is Christ," a "flock of which God himself foretold he would shepherd," a "piece of land to be cultivated, the village of God," and "the dwelling place of God among [human beings]," the document emphasizes the essence of the Church as a mystery whose true form is known only to God (#6).

If the Church is fundamentally a mystery, it logically follows that no particular historical manifestation of the Roman Catholic Church could ever fully express the size and breadth and scope of the "mystical body of Christ." (Recall Augustine's reflection centuries earlier: "There are many whom God has that the Church does not have and many whom the Church has that God does not have.") Thus the true and complete body of Christ "subsists" (LG, #8) in the visible Roman Catholic Church but can never be contained by it.

We are a Church on pilgrimage, ever in need of reform, following the risen Christ who remains now and forever fully present in our midst. The people of God are caught up in the hurricane that is the Holy Spirit who blows forcefully through the visible Roman Catholic Church but can never be contained by it. God sent the Holy Spirit to all humankind to help us love God with our whole heart, soul, mind, and strength and that we might love one another as Christ loves us.

Grace is a waterfall that floods the hearts of all of God's children. Our fundamental vocation as a Christian community is to bear witness to this unconditional love of God that saturates us, "with words, if necessary" as Francis of Assisi said, but primarily through the way in which we live our lives. "The followers of Christ are called by God, not because of their works, but according to his own purpose and grace. They are justified in the Lord Jesus, because in the baptism of faith they truly become sons [and daughters] of God and sharers in the divine nature. In this way, they are really made holy. Then by God's gift, they must hold on to and complete in their lives this holiness they have received" (#40).

A Sign of Contradiction

Vatican Council II came to a close in 1965. The next fifteen years were an exhilarating time of experimentation as the Church sought creative and innovative ways to give flesh to Pope John XXIII's guiding insight: "For the substance of the ancient deposit of faith is one thing, and the way in which it is presented is another." It was a time of deep reflection on the mystery behind the words and actions of the seven sacraments defined by the Council of Trent. Above all else, there was a palpable sense that the rich inner life of the Church could only be incarnated in the world through a renewed commitment by Roman Catholics to stand in solidarity with the "poorest of the poor" by working unceasingly for justice and peace.

When Karol Wojtyla took the name of Pope John Paul II in 1979, the reform movement within the Church inaugurated by the council entered a new phase. Throughout his long pontificate, John Paul II articulated in much greater detail the specifics of this renewed commitment by the Church to solidarity with the poor. He laid out the theological underpinnings of our uncompromising defense of human life. In a world where life is so regularly under assault from abortion, poverty, genocide, slavery, capital punishment, terrorism, nuclear proliferation, fanaticism, discrimination, environmental degradation, and a free market system that too often places profits before the needs of people, John Paul II championed the dignity of every human person.

The pope's role in inspiring the Solidarity movement in Poland will endure as a lasting contribution to the peace and freedom of the modern world. His exhaustive travels to local churches throughout the globe and genuine outreach to the young and to those of other faiths provided a visible witness to the spirit of the document *Guadium et spes* and the increasingly multicultural nature of the Roman Catholic Church. Even the manner in which he died, his last days exuding hope and serenity in the midst of his tremendous suffering, demonstrated that the power of the gospel is so much greater than the power of the forces of cynicism and despair.

The pontificate of John Paul II is a sign of contradiction in another way, however. His progressive advancement of the social justice agenda of the Church was in marked contrast to an extremely conservative if not reactionary attitude toward the decentralization of decision-making and genuine power-sharing within the Church. While the document *Lumen gentium* unambiguously affirmed the pope's authority to make definitive or infallible pronouncements binding on the Church, it did not suggest that this was the ordinary way the doctrine of the Church developed. The document defines the concept of collegiality, that is, just as Peter acted in accord with the rest of the twelve in the early Church, so should the pope act in accord with the rest of the bishops.

Furthermore, the will of the Holy Spirit is most clearly manifested in the Church when there is exhibited a clear unanimity of agreement among clergy, religious. and laity:

> The entire body of the faithful, anointed as they are by the Holy One (cf. John 2:20, 27) cannot err in matters of belief. They manifest this special property by means of the whole people's supernatural discernment in matters of faith when

"from the bishops down to the last of the lay faithful" they show universal agreement in matters of faith and morals. That discernment in matters of faith is aroused and sustained by the Spirit of truth. It is exercised under the guidance of the sacred teaching authority, in faithful and respectful obedience to which the people of God accepts that which is not just the word of men but truly the Word of God. (LG, #12)

Remember that the council devoted an entire chapter of *Lumen gentium* to the unique and essential apostolate of the laity. When coupled with the firmly established social justice principle of Subsidiarity (no higher or more complex form of social organization can usurp the function of a lower, less complex organization), this would suggest that within each diocese and within the universal Church itself there are a wide range of areas—some more practical, such as finance; others more oriented toward the heart of the Church's mission, like catechesis—in which the laity may in fact be more qualified to take active and leading roles than the clergy. In such cases, bishops and individual pastors have a sacred obligation to provide the resources, support, and guidance necessary for the laity to exercise their unique apostolate (LG, #37).

The sex-abuse crisis sadly has demonstrated that forty years after the council there endures within the hierarchy of the Vatican and in many dioceses a strongly entrenched culture of secrecy based on a fundamental mistrust of the laity and a fear of scandal. It is certainly true that the laity has made great strides in taking up a more active ministry within the Church, but it is unclear how much of that change has been the result of proactive efforts on behalf of the universal and local magisterium and how much has occurred by default. Vocations in North America and Western Europe have been declining for at least fifty years, leaving enormous shortages of both priests and religious. Despite the personal charisma of Pope John Paul II and the great admiration both Catholics and non-Catholics have for him, the decline in religious vocations has been matched by a continued decline in regular attendance by the laity in the celebration of the Eucharist. To blame this decline primarily on apathy or a loss of faith among the laity, given the highly centralized and clericalized power structure of the Roman Catholic Church, is something like the police blaming the homeowner who has been tied up inside his house for allowing the robber to take his belongings!

John Paul's decision early in his pontificate to silence the theologians advocating liberation theology in Latin American and others throughout the world sent a chill through the Church. Such actions seemed to reverse the message of Pope John XXIII who wrote: a *process* takes place "when people mutually exchange their perception in the bright light of truth." It's worth noting that if the emperor Constantine returned from the dead some 1700 years later, he would likely feel at home within the hierarchy of the Roman Catholic Church today. As documented at the conclusion of Chapter Three, despite all of the intervening centuries of Church history, the makeup of the central governing authority of the Church—the Roman *Curia*—still looks very much like the governing authority of the Roman Empire. As was true of the governing authority of the empire, the curia remains exclusively male and dependent upon the "Pontifex Maximus" for their appointments. (Remember that in the early Church bishops were chosen by the local church community.) Although Pope John Paul II has spoken out clearly and with great conviction about the dignity of women, he did not take steps to eliminate the sexism within the Church which continues to exclude women from any real participation in the Church policy-making.

In many parishes the laity in general remain at the mercy of pastors who unilaterally decide, often with the bishop's tacit approval, whether or not to consult with or even to allow lay parish councils, despite the clear exhortation in *Lumen gentium* (#37) to do so. Amid the many remarkable attributes that make up the legacy of Pope John Paul II must also be included a festering frustration within the laity that inevitably hampers the emergence of a genuine *sensus fidei* toward the issues of our time both within and without the Church.

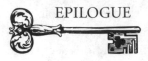

"Be Not Afraid!"

I am not able to conclude this chapter. That conclusion is still being written in the life of the Church. It has been said that it takes three generations to fully implement an ecumenical Church council: the generation of those who attended; the generation of those who were taught by the participants; and the first generation to grow up in a Church that has fully absorbed the vision and decrees of the council. Cardinal Joseph Suenens of Belgium, one of the architects of Vatican Council II, remarked that in about one hundred years he believed the Church would be "very young." Based on these estimates, it seems we still have another generation to go before we can begin to get a sense of what the Church of the third millennium will look like.

In the meantime, we can take comfort from knowing we have been here before, on a number of occasions in fact. Around the time of that first major turning point in Church history, Paul said that all creation was "groaning," waiting to be fully reborn as a result of the death and resurrection of Christ. We live in a time when the *Church* is still groaning, all of us caught in the interval between the death of one way of understanding ourselves and the birth of a new understanding. It is a process that can only be completed according to God's timetable, in Christ and through the Holy Spirit. That Spirit will never be caged by the limitations of our human concepts of Church, but will always appeal to the limitless capacity to love within our hearts.

Matthew's gospel presents a dramatic account in which the disciples of Jesus are in a boat crossing the Sea of Galilee in the midst of a sudden storm. The wind is blowing so forcefully and the waves are so high that the boat can't make any headway. The disciples are unable to see the shoreline. Worst of all, they are on their own; Jesus stayed behind in the mountains to pray. Just when all seems to be lost, something wonderful happens:

> And early in the morning he came walking towards them on the lake. But when the disciples saw him walking on the lake, they were terrified, saying, "It is a ghost!" And they cried out in fear. But immediately Jesus spoke to them and said, "Take heart, it is I; do not be afraid."
>
> Peter answered him, "Lord, if it is you, command me to come to you on the water." He said, "Come." So Peter got out of the boat, started walking on the water, and came towards Jesus. But when he noticed the strong wind, he became frightened, and beginning to sink, he cried out, "Lord, save me!" Jesus immediately reached out his hand and caught him, saying to him, "You of little faith, why did you doubt?" When they got into the boat, the wind ceased. And those in the boat worshiped him, saying, "Truly you are the Son of God." (Matthew 14:22–33)

And so, here we sit. We are tossed about by storms inside and outside the Church. We are unable to see through the tumult the shape and contours of the Church in the third millennium. Frantically we search for Jesus only to discover to our horror and dismay that he is not within the confines of the images of Church with which we are familiar. Yet we need only gaze through the storm with the eyes of faith in order to see what the Holy Spirit sees. There the risen Christ stands, at the center of the Church and at the center of time and of space, upholding and infusing all creation with his presence. He beckons to us to walk toward him, beyond our fears and our limitations, beyond even the farthest reaches of our rational minds. It seems that when we respond, we are defying the very laws of nature. In fact, we are transcending them.

What I fervently hope and pray this book has demonstrated is that throughout our history the core of the Christian faith is always a personal and communal relationship with the risen Christ. The core of *Catholic* Christian spirituality is a recognition that, through the Incarnation, all of creation has been sanctified. There are as many pathways to Christ as there are particular callings of the Spirit.

We have been here before. The howling wind is really the voice of the Spirit, calling us to change our course once again and to follow Jesus to new shores. Our commitment to the journey—whether we actually reach those shores or not—is the greatest legacy we can leave to our children and grandchildren.

Onward.

For Thought and Discussion

1) What do you think the Church of the third millennium will look like?

2) What are the signs of hope you see in the present? Signs of concern?

3) Here are some thoughts from my own high school students, given in response to the question, "What are the qualities of an ideal family?" It struck me that many of their answers held precious insights that might help all of us discern the movement of the Spirit in the Church today more clearly.

   • "An ideal family would be able to spend time with one another as well as pray together and get along. An ideal family would also work together to help other families or people in need."

   • "The ideal family would respect each member's actions, beliefs, and requests. A family should love each other for who they are and not for their special talents."

   • "To me, a family should be a close group of people brought together by blood and kept together by love. Families should be the people we always rely on for help, not the people we run from and cause us to seek help."

   • "The ideal family brings one another to a place of goodness in their hearts."

- "A true model family would be one that demonstrates unconditional love. This idea originates from the way in which Jesus
  himself behaved toward everyone he encountered."

What is your definition?

4) Describe some of the historical developments that led to Pius IX
   "syllabus of errors." Did Pius IX overreact or did he err on the side
   of caution?

5) What are the five basic principles of Catholic social justice theory
   outlined in this chapter? Explain how one principle or several principles apply to an important modern-day moral issue. (Example,
   global economic or environmental displacement.)

6) What is the importance of the Vatican II Council? How do the
   Council's teaching challenge us to rethink the nature of the
   Church?

Suggested Readings

My goal in writing this book was to give a basic sense of what a dynamic, colorful, and, ultimately sacramental community the Church truly is. For further reading about the adventures of the body of Christ and more particular and comprehensive information about the people, movements, and ideas mentioned here, I recommend the following sources.

Invaluable Resources

Women in Church History by Joanne Turpin (St. Anthony Messenger Press, 1989) presents twenty stories—one for each century—of women who have made important and lasting contributions to the Church and the world. It is a necessary and wonderfully written corrective to the usual male dominated parade of saints and sinners in other Church history texts.

Catholic Customs and Traditions by Greg Dues (Twenty-Third Publications, revised 2002) is a compendium of everything you have ever wanted to know about, well, catholic customs and traditions and how they developed into the forms we know them by today. I am particularly indebted to Greg for his treatment of indulgences.

General Overviews

A Concise History of the Catholic Church by Thomas Bokenkotter (Image Books, Doubleday, 1978) is the most thorough and most readable overview from a Catholic perspective that I have come across, and it is widely used.

Paul Johnson's *History of Christianity*, reprinted by Simon and Schuster's Touchstone books in 2005, is another good source, this time from a Protestant perspective.

For an even more concise overview, I recommend either *The Catholic Church: A Brief History* by Alfred Lapple (Paulist Press, 1977) or *The Catholic Church: Journey, Wisdom, and Mission* by Carl Koch (St. Mary's Press, revised 1995).

Specific Time Periods

Anthony E. Gilles's *The People of...* series (St. Anthony Messenger Press) contains volumes corresponding to key eras in the history of the Church and its Hebrew roots. They include: *The People of the Book* (Old Testament times); *The People of the Way* (New Testament times); *The People of the Creed* (early Church); *The People of the Faith* (medieval Church); *The People of Anguish* (the Reformation), and *The People of Hope* (the modern Church). Mr. Gilles fresh approach to Church history, clearly informed by *Lumen gentium*, the document on the Church promulgated at the Vatican Council II, was an important source for this book and an inspiration to me to try and find a new angle of my own.

To gain some further insight into the early centuries of the Christian story, try *The Early Church* by W.H.C. Frend (Fortress Press, 1982). I have never read a better effort of synthesizing ancient and obscure Christian writings into a readable format. Augustine's *Confessions* provides an introduction to the mind of a great bishop and theologian as well as some indirect insight into the Church during the final days of the Western Roman Empire.

To get a sense of the Church in the medieval period, I would recommend Chaucer's *Canterbury Tales* and Dante's *Divine Comedy*, in particular *Inferno*. Although they are works of fiction, both writers succeed in capturing the "feel" of the period in ways works of history never could.

For two very different views of the modern Church, try *101 Questions and Answers on Vatican II* by Maureen Sullivan, OP (Paulist Press, 2002) and *Structures of Deceit: Papal Sin* by Garry Wills (Doubleday, 2000). Sr. Sullivan gives a concise and easy-to-read overview of the history, accomplishments, and legacy of the council, and along the way, she offers insights into modern developments of Catholic theology. Mr. Wills looks at the other side of the story, in a sense at the contradictions within the teachings of the Church brought to light by the council but which have yet to be resolved.

As to the future, read *Catholicism in the Third Millennium* by Thomas Rausch (Liturgical Press, 2003). Fr. Rausch sketches a comprehensive and intriguing vision of what the Church of the next millennium might look like. *Why Christianity Must Change or Die* by Episcopalian Bishop John Shelby Spong (HarperCollins, 1998) is another provocative reflection on the future of the Church.

Primary Sources

If you want to dispense with the intermediaries and delve directly into the historical sources themselves, most of the writings mentioned in this book, such as *The Cloud of Unknowing*, Thomas' *Summa Theologiae* or *The Interior Castle* by Teresa of Avila are generally available in inexpensive editions. Try Image Books—an imprint of Doubleday—which is now a division of Random House, for starters.

William A. Jurgens is the author of the classic compilation of Christian writings which have survived the collapse of the Western Roman Empire, the works of the so-called Church Fathers. They are available through Liturgical Press. *The First Seven Ecumenical Councils (325–787): Their History and Theology* by Leo D. Davis, SJ, is also available through Liturgical Press.

To obtain copies of any of the papal encyclicals quoted in this book from the time of Leo XIII to the present, contact Pauline Books and Media or download directly from the Vatican website: www.vatican.va/offices/papal_docs_list.html. Documents are listed in alphabetical order.

To obtain copies of documents produced by the United States Conference of Catholic Bishops, including "The Challenge of Peace," go to www.usccb.org.

And now for something completely different…

Once A Catholic by Peter Occhiogrosso (Houghton Mifflin Co., 1987) is the most unusual source I used in seeking to get a sense of the Church in the modern world. It consists of a series of interviews with Catholics—some lapsed, some practicing, some famous, some not. The reflections Mr. Occhiogrosso has gathered run the gamut from the more progressive thoughts of Joan Chittister, OSB ("Someplace along the line, we are going to have to become more a Church of questions than of answers"), to the conservative ideas of Michael Novak ("The benefit of the doubt lies with the mystery of the papacy"), to the one-of-a-kind musings of the late rock star Frank Zappa ("I tell my daughter that whenever anyone says they want to talk to her about Jesus to get away as fast as possible").